MW01063862

THE ECHO MACHINE

THE ECHO MACHINE

HOW RIGHT-WING EXTREMISM
CREATED A POST-TRUTH AMERICA

DAVID PAKMAN

Beacon Press • Boston

Beacon Press
Boston, Massachusetts
www.beacon.org

Beacon Press books
are published under the auspices of
the Unitarian Universalist Association of Congregations.

28   27   26   25 | 8   7   6   5   4   3   2   1

This book is printed on acid-free paper that meets the uncoated paper ANSI/NISO
specifications for permanence as revised in 1992.

Text design by BookMatters

Library of Congress Cataloguing-in-Publication Data is available for this title.
Hardcover ISBN: 978-0-8070-1653-4
E-book ISBN: 978-0-8070-1654-1
Audiobook: 978-0-8070-1827-9

CONTENTS

WHY I HATE POLITICS

The American political space is toxic. When I explain in private conversations that I dislike politics, it often surprises people to hear it. Indeed, declaring in a political book that I "hate" politics is admittedly odd. One would reasonably imagine that the host of a political talk show would "like" politics. However, the specifics of this dislike are the critical detail.

While I care deeply both about the future of the country and planet, and about the issues that are regularly topics of discussion on *The David Pakman Show*, the hate is focused elsewhere. The aspect of politics I hate is that those who want to engage with the political system to make progress and improve the lives of people in the US and around the world end up needlessly bogged down by pointless fights and disagreements over the difference between fact and opinion, or arguing about issues where there is an empirical consensus among experts, including climate change, the disastrous impact of the "war on drugs" when compared to the efficacy of harm reduction strategies in drug policy, or the scientific reality about vaccines.

One of the great pleasures of producing and hosting a political talk program is the nearly instantaneous feedback that comes in from the audience. Sadly, much of that feedback is uninformed, based on information that is incorrect. And this gets us to the crux of the matter: opting out of the political system because it is such an infuriating environment will only make the problem worse. Existing political participation allows the disastrous ideas from the ignorant and ill-intentioned to go unchallenged in culture and potentially be unopposed legislatively. But as we're quickly learning, to engage in politics, at least in the United States, is to engage with reactionary and ignorant right-wing movements, as well as often well-intentioned but misinformed political allies on the Left.

For example, take climate change. Because we have science deniers among our ranks, rather than channeling and focusing creativity and resources into solving the climate crisis, energy, time, and resources have to instead be spent pushing against those who refuse to accept uncontroversial science about what is taking place on our planet. Rather than making real, rapid progress to get away from dirty and polluting energy sources as quickly as possible, we have to spend precious time responding to people who believe that a cold winter day is proof that there's nothing to worry about. We are wasting time debating people who don't think abortion should be legal, or that two men shouldn't be able to get legally married.

Cultural critics, sociologists, futurists, and technologists alike have pointed out that modern media, technology, and consumer culture are often most pernicious in that they tell us not necessarily what to think, but what to think about. Much the same way, one of the major frustrations of engaging with the American political space is that we are wasting time having to fight against the tired, debunked notions that others continue to think about.

It's difficult to remain calm when we realize how much we are missing in our ability to make progress when the vast majority of the discourse is not focused on the major issues of our time. Are we as a human race on earth advanced enough, able enough, and wealthy enough that we can end abject poverty and human suffering and ensure that our entire global population is, at a minimum, housed and fed? Every serious study says that the answer is yes, but what is lacking is the political will. When the debate is focused on, for example, "lazy" unemployed people and food stamps, it's difficult to solve big problems of unfair inequality. Instead of having a society and species focused on solving the problem, we are relegated to arguing with people who will not even accept that this is a problem needing a solution, and that's the reality of the political world that I hate.

There may be no way around this. To change the system, one must engage with the system. The alternative is to bury one's head in the sand, guaranteeing that nothing will be accomplished, other than allowing those with the worst instincts and most disastrous ideas to make all of the decisions, a tragic and devastating outcome. The only result guaranteed by that surrender is that those with the worst ideas determine the future of humanity, and that cannot be allowed.

Engaging with American politics has always been a unique experience, characterized by highs and lows and by the revolutionary nature of the founding of the country. Historically, the United States has seen periods of intense political activism and enthusiasm followed by phases of disillusionment and cynicism. Understanding this fluctuating engagement is crucial to contextualizing our present predicament.

The birth of the nation was fueled by revolutionary zeal. Town hall meetings and discussions were common, and engagement was high. Colonists passionately discussed and debated the merits of independence from Britain. This early political engagement was not just about breaking away, but about the enthusiasm for crafting a new, ideally just and representative system.

In the lead-up to and after the Civil War, there was a newfound sense of purpose to rebuild and restructure. Black Americans especially engaged politically, voting and even holding public offices. But this surge was short-lived, as the introduction of Jim Crow laws suppressed their voices and votes. This connects to the story unpacked in chapter 1 about the role of the civil rights era in ushering in the fracturing of our politics.

Known as the Progressive Era, the late nineteenth and early twentieth centuries saw another spike in political activism, this one leading to great progressive victories. Concerned citizens, alarmed by the increasing influence of big businesses and rampant corruption, called for reforms. It was an era of muckrakers, suffragists, and labor activists.

After World War II, the US experienced an economic boom and a surge in civic engagement, following the New Deal and leading up to the Civil Rights Movement. Anti–Vietnam War protests and other activist movements showed a politically engaged population very much ready to challenge the status quo. But since then, we've seen a decline in enthusiasm, which manifests in more ways than simply apathy about participating in elections.

The cynicism brought in by Watergate in the 1970s disillusioned and demotivated many from engagement with politics and generated a new distrust of those in power and our institutions. As we approached the year 2000, there was dwindling election turnout as voters, including young people, felt their voice wouldn't make a difference. This is directly intertwined with the Bush era.

Most recently, while the Internet and social media at least theoretically opened the door to a more connected and informed citizenry, we have seen division and radicalization increase, without truly increasing productive political engagement. The rise of echo chambers and misinformation has made constructive dialogue difficult if not impossible, and comparisons to other countries don't provide a reason for optimism.

Comparing American political engagement with other countries is both enlightening and depressing. For instance, Scandinavian countries like Sweden and Denmark often see voter turnouts of above 80 percent, attributed to their proportional representation systems and high levels of trust in their governments. In the US, even in general elections—"significant" ones, as if any are insignificant—turnout rarely exceeds 60 percent. There are many reasons for this higher level of engagement in Scandinavian countries.

Sweden and Denmark both use proportional representation systems, where political parties gain seats in proportion to their share of the popular vote. This ensures that every voter's vote contributes to the ultimate makeup of their legislative bodies. In the United States, all that matters is which candidate gets the most votes within their particular district or race, and nothing else. Thus, 49 percent of the voters in every district could conceivably end up with none of their first—and only—choices representing them.

To a degree, lower turnout in the US also relates to a lack of tradition and responsibility attached to voting. Although attitudes have changed over time, in the modern political era—certainly in the twenty-first century—not voting, not engaging, and not being informed do not have the negative connotation that they once did. I often remark that political discussion is much rarer in American society than in, for example, my birth country of Argentina. In Argentina, politics invariably comes up as a topic with one's cab driver, clothing store salesperson, or restaurant waitstaff. In the US, this is not only less common socially and culturally, but often looked down upon on the basis that "religion and politics" are private topics, not to be discussed in polite society.

Another aspect to low engagement in the US comes from low trust in government, and low confidence that one's policy preferences will actually be made into law. In the Scandinavian model, there is more transparency, less corruption, and more cooperation in governments to deliver on the actual policy priorities of the voters.

The grass is not always greener on the other side. There are examples of developed countries that struggle with political engagement. Japan, for example, has a stable democracy, yet still has widespread political apathy. Young citizens are particularly disengaged, and this is a problem that goes beyond voting, with widespread concerns about young Japanese who choose to be celibate and often do not socialize at all, relegating themselves to their homes to a degree that has become a public health issue. Often this disconnection is blamed on a Japanese educational system that does not encourage civic responsibility and engagement. However, there is hope—dating back to Reiwa Shinsengumi's success in 2019—that a turnaround will happen.

Overall, political engagement across the world is complex. What can be said definitively is that while the US is not at the bottom, much is left to be desired.

One of the most relevant aspects of this discussion of disenfranchisement and widespread misinformation is the changing role that media, including news media and social media, have had in shaping the political status quo in the United States.

The American media landscape has shifted dramatically. What used to be the domination of newspapers and radio broadcasts has given way to twenty-four-hour cable news, omnipresent digital platforms, and fragmented and polarizing social media networks.

The algorithm-driven platforms curate content based on user behavior and preexisting preferences. This machinery leads to echo chambers, filter bubbles, and the reinforcement of existing points of view, while marginalizing contrasting viewpoints, even if the contrasting viewpoints are the ones based in fact. Not only does this polarize society and diminish the ability of the population to engage with disagreement, but it promotes misinformation as truth, circulating unverified and often debunked claims in these closed loops, with no way to break the cycle.

The line between news and entertainment has been as blurred as ever, particularly since the advent of Fox News in 1996. Sensational stories and opinion pieces are produced and packaged in a way that looks like news reporting. Journalism is diluted, fun is prioritized over fact, and discerning reality is even more difficult for audiences.

Within this highly radicalized, undereducated, propagandized environment, misinformation and disinformation run rampant. Misinformation—unintentionally false information—spreads due to ignorance, while disinformation—deliberately false information—is spread by bad actors. The end result is not only the spread of false information itself. The realization that some information being popularly shared is false generates a general distrust in all reporting and news sources, making it even easier for individuals to dismiss any reporting they don't like as "fake news," or disinformation, even if it is truly accurate.

Part of this can be explained by economic factors and by news media being a business. The need for advertising revenue and strangled budgets for investigative journalism leave many media outlets to figure out how to generate the largest audience at the lowest possible cost.

At the same time, the lack of media literacy, addressed in our discussions of education and elsewhere in the book, becomes a critical reinforcing problem. Better-educated audiences would be better equipped to navigate the media terrain, including social media, to avoid falling for and ultimately signal-boosting mis- and disinformation. Understanding the economic incentives of media outlets would also help. Unfortunately, the American right wing benefits from the lack of media literacy. Their narratives disproportionately depend on spreading mis- and disinformation. This explains why Republicans have defunded and outright eliminated critical thinking and media literacy classes from public school curricula around the country.

As a result of this fractured and broken political system, immersion in the political landscape can exact a heavy personal toll. For me, it's not an abstract possibility but a daily reality. Hosting a political talk show means not only being informed about the latest political developments but also confronting the most extreme manifestations of the nation's polarization. The constant barrage of vitriolic feedback, disparaging comments, and even outright threats can wear down even the most resilient spirit. The fervor of political fanaticism often diverts attention from the human being behind the microphone, leading to a kind of dehumanization that can be deeply disheartening. As a result, as I've discussed with my audience, I restrict my engagement with "the news" to only the days of the week on which I produce programming, and deliberately exclude it from my media diet on other days.

A feeling of despondency can be common among media consumers. Politics starts to seem more like a circus than a vehicle for change and for improving the lives of citizens. Followers of the news begin to feel like spectators who are powerless to effect change. When elected officials prioritize scoring political points, and studies regularly find that the policy priorities of the wealthy and of corporations are what politicians are most likely to make reality, this feeling only grows.

Cynicism develops from a mere defense mechanism against disappointment into the default stance for many, so acute that some simply opt out altogether. Politicians make promises, fail to deliver on them, and blame someone else. Corrosive cynicism spreads from doubt about individual politicians to doubt about our democracy overall. We find ourselves caught in the echo machine. This has the feedback-loop effect of impeding genuine grassroots movements that fail to take off because of the initial cynicism, and thus ultimately fail to prevent the erosion of the foundations of our democracy.

Individual mental health is also on the line. Anxiety and depression rates have been on the rise, with many contributing factors. The widespread availability of smartphones on which social media can be accessed hundreds of times per day is one component. Salacious or particularly fear-based news is more likely to "go viral" and be shared and reshared on these very platforms. The ever-present dread of "what's next," a collective doomscrolling, makes it difficult to escape this pervasive sense of despondency. The feeling of impotence about effecting change only contributes to the mental health decline.

In addition to catalyzing negative emotions from a mental health standpoint, this emotional toll includes suppressing positive emotions as well. The narrative perpetuated by polarized and radicalized news media and social media creates an atmosphere in which typically empathetic individuals burn out, start to lose empathy, and become fatigued enough to give up. An "activism fatigue" takes hold, especially when tangible change seems elusive and pushes us away from advocating, protesting, and resisting.

In the end, the strong emotional component of American politics leads to personal suffering and a suppression of activism. Even activists who feel energized by this regrettable status quo can become frustrated when extremist messages drown out productive moderate voices. It is understandable that such an environment is not sustainable and will push away more people than it draws in.

I strongly make the case that not engaging is not an option—at least not a productive and viable option that will improve society. Despite being frustrating and demoralizing, engaging in the political process, even when it seems Sisyphean, is a critical method for instigating change. History is replete with instances where sustained grassroots activism led to significant social and political transformations that initially seemed impossible. From the Civil Rights Movement to recent global initiatives tackling climate change, it is evident that collective action has the power to challenge the status quo and drive progress. Disengagement, on the other hand, cedes ground to the status quo and diminishes the potential for reform. It's also worth considering that political systems and processes are not static; they evolve in response to participation and pressure. By staying engaged, individuals can contribute to the gradual reshaping of the political landscape in ways that align more closely with their visions for a just and equitable society. As easy as it is to become disillusioned and end up "hating" politics, it's essential to continue participating in our political world, with voting being the starting point and catalyst for that engagement.

Too frequently, nonfiction political books take a decidedly pessimistic tone, presenting societal problems as both insurmountable and inevitable while spending very little time proposing a list of solutions. The solutions on those lists tend to be so unlikely, complicated, and overwhelming that entire books could be written about each. This book will be different. Without a doubt, there is much to be pessimistic and concerned about, but we will focus on identifying problems so that they can be solved, rather than generating a doom spiral. The history and path taken to get us to this point will be explored, the specific pain points and problems will be identified, and a framework for improvement and solutions will be outlined.

CHAPTER 1

HOW THE UNITED STATES BROKE

I t is often said that American politics is broken, that there is something about our political system that at some point worked, but stopped working. In reality, the problem is even greater: American politics is indeed broken, but so are American economics, culture, and education. To understand how we might change this demoralizing status quo, we will first seek to understand what broke it in the first place.

Some readers may find this story new, while others may already be familiar with it. The takeaway should be one of cautious optimism in that—fortunately—we know what broke the country. Another source of realistic optimism is that not all is bad in the United States of America. Yet it is far easier to find examples of what is not working than of what is. The flourishing of some does not diminish the suffering of others, and functional elements of society don't invalidate elements that do not work.

My hope is that this chapter and this story will, at some point in the not-too-distant future, be a reminder of how things used to be rather than the continued status quo. It would be a great pleasure to look back at a time when our political and economic conditions were as broken as they are today as a bygone era of how things used to be, rather than as the storm in which we find ourselves actually.

When we discuss a breakage, we are referring to the wholesale and multifaceted degradation over a period of several decades, visible in numerous foundational areas. They all relate to the promise and idea of the United States of America: the dream of equal opportunity, the once-apparently-unbreakable tenets of democracy, the storied principle of all individuals having the right to life, liberty, and the pursuit of happiness. Much of this has been repeated and enumerated before.

The fracture, however, is evidenced in many areas. One can look pointedly at income inequality data, or a chart comparing historical wages to inflation and productivity.[1] One can zoom out and consider more broadly the erosion of workers' rights, the undermining of democratic norms and institutions, and the attempts to break our democracy itself.[2]

This deterioration was not abrupt, nor was it carried out by one group of individuals. It was not even carried out deliberately in the sense of a "grand plan" in many cases. It has been a culmination of successive events, political maneuvering, cynicism, greed, and systemic failures over time. In some instances, it's linked to the ascendancy of corporate interests over the rights of individuals.[3]

This has all been compounded by the additional layers of the distorted mass media and, more recently, social media ecosystem, as well as educational systems that are failing—in some cases by design—in parts of the country. The result is a widening chasm between reality and perception for many Americans.

There is reasonable disagreement about exactly when this began. In some sense, it began when the United States began, or even earlier, through the self-selection bias of those who chose to come to settle the US in the first place.

There is no exact science to starting this exploration in the mid- to late 1950s. One could look earlier, for example, to the fight for women's voting rights that started to some degree in the 1800s but exploded in the early twentieth century, culminating in women's suffrage succeeding in 1919 with the Nineteenth Amendment to the US Constitution, later ratified in 1920.

For our purposes, in considering the modern political environment and the problems we identify and seek to solve, we will start our story of this breakage around the civil rights era. There are two primary reasons why this serves as a useful starting point:

1. Reactionary elements in the United States more openly started to resist the push toward a more inclusive country at this time.[4]

2. The pre–civil rights era of the early 1950s remains an emblematic "golden era" for many modern American reactionaries, the "good ol' days" to which many want to return.[5]

In other chapters, we'll consider other time periods, but for now, we start in the late 1950s.

The Civil Rights Movement gained momentum in the late 1950s and into the first half of the 1960s, culminating at least in some immediate legal sense with the Civil Rights Act of 1964. In the strongly segregated and discriminatory United States of America up to that point, leaders such as Dr. Martin Luther King Jr., Mrs. Rosa Parks, Malcolm X, and others became icons of a struggle to secure equal rights under the law for all Americans, regardless of race.

One need not agree with every tactic or method employed by every figure in this fight to recognize that the surging opposition to the Civil Rights Movement contained deeply rooted beliefs in White supremacy and the desire to maintain the status quo for those whom it benefited. Most societal shifts bring resistance and pushback, and the civil rights era was no exception.

Our exploration is less about the civil rights era itself, and more about the role that opposition played in developing the American right wing into its later forms, including MAGA Trumpism and beyond.

Many White business owners in the South worried that desegregation would be damaging economically, by virtue of White customers boycotting their businesses if they served Black customers or hired Black employees.[6] The social hierarchy that existed in much of the South, deeply entrenched at the time, risked being upended by desegregation.

Some, in particular among religious White communities, opposed integrations and civil rights on religious or moral grounds. As has been the case in the battles for LGBTQ+ rights, abortion rights, and other rights, this group would often cite biblical justifications for racial separation. Whether these citations were accurate is irrelevant, as using religious texts to justify civil law clearly violates the principle of separation of church and state on which the United States was founded.

More generally, social change can cause fear, and fear is unsettling. Some neuroscience research has found that reactionary right-wingers

have larger fear centers in their brains and are more likely to be motivated by fear,[7] and on this basis, it is predictable and consistent that
right-wingers would have been more afraid of the Civil Rights Movement, and therefore more strident in their opposition.

Much as the twenty-first century has seen, the general fear of communism also played a role in the twentieth century, including in fomenting
opposition to the civil rights era. Some conservatives equated the entire
movement with communism, arguing that civil rights activists were being
manipulated by communists or were communists themselves.[8]

Lastly, some opposed these changes on the basis of "states' rights"
and the idea that the federal government was overstepping its bounds by
forcing states to desegregate schools and other public institutions. This
rings relatively similar to those who argued that the Civil War was not
about slavery but, coincidentally, also about states' rights—states' rights
to continue having slaves. An evaluation of the sincerity of the concern
leaves most reasonable observers unimpressed with their truth.

The Civil Rights Movement to some degree culminated in the Civil
Rights Act of 1964. Despite widespread discrimination continuing, our
narrative follows the political story, and the undercurrent of opposition
in the aftermath of the act's passing became increasingly vocal. Southern Whites claimed "alienation" and a nostalgic yearning for "how things
used to be," meaning the early to mid-1950s before the civil rights era.
The self-proclaimed disenfranchised needed someone to help organize
them and be their voice, and that someone was Ronald Reagan.

By the time Ronald Reagan's 1980 presidential campaign got underway
in earnest with a televised speech from New York City in 1979, antipathy
for "the direction the country is going" as a result of the civil rights era
was at a fever pitch. During the early 1970s, the feeling that the country
was in a state of "flux" and instability was perceivable not only through
tension surrounding the expansion of civil rights for minority groups but
also through uncertainty about and growing opposition to the Vietnam
War. The scandal surrounding President Richard Nixon and Watergate,
which in some sense ended on August 8, 1974, when Nixon announced his
resignation on national television, furthered this sense of "and now what?"

Conservatives and the American Right seized on this directional ambiguity by arguing what the country needed was a return to "traditional"

American values, now a well-known and transparent dog whistle to a time lacking equality of opportunity, equality under the law, and gender equality while discrimination of all kinds ran rampant.

Republican Ronald Reagan, having previously been the governor of California, seized on this hankering for "traditional" values, making a critical element of his 1980 campaign a hostility to social welfare programs.[9] Reagan painted the US government as being too big, inefficient, and intrusive in people's lives.[10] Anecdotal stories quickly became a centerpiece for Reagan in illustrating this view, in order to score political points and position himself as exactly what conservatives had been looking for.

One of the most famous and controversial anecdotes was that of the "welfare queen" who drove a Cadillac, persistently pregnant in order to secure additional welfare money through the birthing of ever more babies. This story, told by Reagan to an audience in Asheville, North Carolina, in January 1976, was the result of a Reagan adviser finding a wire story about Linda Taylor, identified by the *Chicago Tribune* in 1974 after committing welfare fraud. She indeed did drive a Cadillac and became the example that created the stereotype.

This story was racially tinged—Taylor was Black—and sought to portray welfare programs as being riddled with fraud and available for cheats to take advantage of. The point was to frame welfare programs as wasteful and pointless, and those receiving benefits as lazy and dishonest. Overall, Reagan helped mobilize the American Right against welfare programs, and coddled implicitly racist and xenophobic ideas through the imagery he used. More than anything else, Taylor's story is a sign of the necessity of increasing access to health care, including mental health care, a policy position that Republicans have come to oppose over recent decades.[11]

In viewing Reagan as the link between the reaction to the Civil Rights Act and the further radicalization of Republicans when Newt Gingrich became Speaker of the House in 1994, the other important elements to consider are Reagan's economic policies and his broader social conservatism.

"Reaganomics," as it became known, depended greatly on the belief in trickle-down economics, premised on the concept that reducing taxes for the wealthiest would stimulate the economy, thus "trickling down" and benefiting all economic classes. The typical mechanism cited by believers in this idea is that by cutting taxes on the rich, it will encourage them to reinvest in their businesses, hire more employees, and spend on other related activities. Although there can be elements of this that are theoretically logical, some—for example, hiring employees simply because you received a tax cut—make no sense. Businesses hire employees based on demand for their products and services, not because the owners received a tax cut. Additionally, since business expenses ("investing in your business") are tax deductible, reducing taxable income, it is further counterintuitive to imagine stimulating investment by cutting taxes for owners.

George H. W. Bush followed Ronald Reagan as president and ultimately lost his reelection campaign to Bill Clinton in 1992. The political constituency that welcomed Reagan's ideological package was furious about Clinton's win. In 1994, ready and waiting to be further radicalized, Newt Gingrich became Speaker of the House of Representatives.

Bill Clinton's 1992 victory greatly galvanized Republicans and pushed them even further to the right. President Clinton's policies seem absolutely moderate in comparison to the political climate of the country in the 2020s, but despite this, the animosity toward Clinton for being "far left" was palpable. This sentiment resulted in massive Republican gains in the 1994 midterm election. Republicans won the national popular vote for the House of Representatives by a margin of 6.8 percentage points and picked up fifty-four seats in the House, as well as eight in the Senate. Republicans selected Newt Gingrich, who had been in the House of Representatives since winning in the 1978 election, to be Speaker of the House.

Gingrich's reign marked the aggressive weaponization of government tools against ideological opponents, with Bill Clinton being the primary target. It also set the next stage of radicalization, leading to the presidency of George W. Bush.

Building on the "hankering" for conservative values that buoyed Reagan, Republicans under the leadership of Newt Gingrich sought to unify their messaging and appeal to voters in a new and groundbreaking way. They concocted the "Contract with America,"[12] a concise document that encapsulated a broad conservative vision and promised swift legislative action within the first hundred days of a Republican-controlled Congress. This worked.

The full scope of the contract is not acutely relevant to our story, but the general direction of it should be understood. Ideas that became Republican orthodoxy by the time of the George W. Bush era, and persisted under President Obama into MAGA Trumpism, originated under Gingrich's leadership. The idea of "balancing the budget" as a priority was outlined in the Fiscal Responsibility Act. A focus on tougher crime laws, including increased prison funding, harsher penalties, and more aggressive policing, appeared under the heading of the Taking Back Our Streets Act. The focus on welfare "reform," actually ways to gut welfare programs, gained momentum under the Personal Responsibility Act.

Republicans in the 1990s happily used government tools for political gain, notably through their weaponization of government against President Clinton. The Whitewater controversy started as an investigation into the real estate investments of the Clintons with the Whitewater Development Corporation. Originating in the area of financial matters, under independent counsel Ken Starr, it expanded into a sprawling fishing expedition that included the firing of White House travel agents and the alleged misuse of FBI files.

Then came the impeachment proceedings against President Clinton, related to news of Clinton's affair with White House intern Monica Lewinsky. Clinton's initial dishonest denial of the affair led to a full-blown impeachment push by Republicans who claimed that Clinton committed perjury during his deposition in the Paula Jones lawsuit, where he denied the affair with Lewinsky. In December 1998, the House of Representatives approved two articles of impeachment against Clinton: perjury and obstruction of justice.

As is the case in presidential impeachments, a trial was conducted in the Senate, where the ultimate vote did not lead to a conviction and removal from office for President Clinton, acquitting him of both charges in 1999.

The Whitewater investigation and Clinton impeachment were in fact similar to what Donald Trump later claimed to be experiencing. Governmental processes of oversight and checks and balances were wielded as political weapons, putting aside what was best for the country and its voters. This laid the groundwork for future debasement along the same lines.

One additional aspect to the mid-1990s was massively consequential, as we'll soon see: Fox News went on the air in 1996, causing a shift in the media landscape, pushing the rise of cable news as a source of political agenda-setting, and becoming an irreversible radicalizing force in American politics and culture.

During Gingrich's reign, the foundation was laid for increasingly segmented and polarized news consumption. It did not rise to anywhere near the severity of the twenty-first century in the era of YouTube, podcasts, and social media, but it did start the country in that direction. Importantly, despite Fox News still being in its infancy at the end of the 1990s, its influence began to extend beyond television and its immediate audience. Fox News narratives, in conjunction with talk radio hosts such as Rush Limbaugh, often set the tone and agenda for conservative positions, ensuring that those perspectives reached a broad audience across multiple media forms.

Now several decades into the extremist slide of the Republican Party, we arrive at the presidency of George W. Bush. Putting aside commentary about Bush himself with regard to intellectual curiosity and cognitive ability, the Bush era saw the most overt celebration of anti-intellectualism up to that point. While it fell well short of what ultimately developed under President Donald Trump, it was a decidedly notable turn.[13]

The Republicans of the time, in their best effort to run interference for the obvious celebration of being against critical thinking, academia, and deep research, attempted to put a positive spin on their movement by emphasizing that their political positions were simply "common sense." This was framed as a contrast to the "elite" viewpoints that were out of touch with the average American, or the academic perspectives that were simply a version of left-wing indoctrination, to be ignored and marginalized. This theme loomed increasingly larger over the discourse as Bush gave way to Obama, and eventually to Trump.

A significant catalyst for this approach came from Bush's cultivation of appearing to be an "average guy," despite having an Ivy League education and an elite background, and coming from a family political dynasty of the highest order. Bush pushed imagery of clearing brush at his ranch in Texas, attending baseball games, and of being a man known for simple and plain speech rather than intellectualism. Despite Bush's actual background, the Republican Party of this era successfully built support for the views that college educations were liberal indoctrination, that liberal political opponents were out-of-touch elites or coastal intellectuals, and that their views could and likely should be ignored.

Under Bush, Republicans had not yet completely abandoned policy, which they did implicitly during President Obama's two terms, and explicitly during Donald Trump's presidential campaign and eventual presidency. When it came to diplomacy, the idea was "you're either with us or against us," and this was used to manufacture consent for the misguided Iraq War—a war based on faulty intelligence[14]—by positioning opponents to the war as unpatriotic, or even sympathetic to the enemies of the United States, whoever they were understood to be in that moment.

Dangerously, an unmistakable dismissal of scientific consensus was popularized by the Bush Republican movement. Whether it was climate change or stem cell research,[15] scientific viewpoints were often ignored or pushed aside in policy decisions, and it became increasingly acceptable to replace science and empiricism with mere opinion, or sometimes with religious texts.[16]

In addition to the anti-intellectualism of this era, another critical aspect was the promotion and embrace of simple, obvious solutions to problems. This relates to a far broader issue of political messaging and language, written about extensively by George Lakoff, Thomas Frank, and others. Suffice it to say, the Bush era trained and predisposed Republicans to favor simple solutions, often derived from oversimplifications of issues. Such examples include:

- Taxes are bad because it's your money. Why shouldn't you get to keep it?
- Abortion ends a life. It should be illegal.
- The planet has been here a long time and it's huge. Humans couldn't possibly be able to affect the climate. We don't need to worry about that.

This through line of prioritizing simplicity over nuanced, deep understanding of issues was ultimately critical in building opposition to much of what then-future President Obama and the Democrats would come to propose from 2009 to 2017.

The Obama era is an important next stop in understanding the radicalization of the Republican Party and the fracture of the United States not only because of the racist and xenophobic reaction to President Barack Obama, but also because of vice presidential candidate Sarah Palin serving as a perfect bridge between the soft anti-intellectualism of George

W. Bush and the aggressive, weaponized delusions of MAGA Trumpism. Let's discuss each in parts.

President Barack Obama's mother was White and his father was Black. This makes Obama half Black, or half White—multiracial. Culturally, however, Barack Obama was a Black man, and this was immediately influential in the response he generated from the American right wing. The election of President Obama was without question a sign of progress of a sort in the United States, and it also became a mirror that reflected the country's long-standing racial animosities.

One of the most pervasive and racially charged accusations against Obama was the birther movement, which claimed that he was not born in the United States. This was partially "merely" racism and xenophobia, but it was also used to suggest that Obama was actually an illegitimate president and not entitled to hold the office. Despite Obama releasing his long-form birth certificate in 2011, this conspiracy theory lingered, pushed by notable figures including future president Donald Trump.[17] In fact, promoting birtherism was likely responsible, in part, for setting Trump up for a successful Republican presidential primary run in 2016. At its core, the birther movement was a sinister attempt to undermine America's first Black president, casting doubt on his authenticity as an American.

The gravity of the racial animosity that Obama faced was underscored by the increasingly brazen and public nature of overtly racist commentary about Obama. The Obama era did not create racism, but Obama's presence in the Oval Office as a half-Black man disinhibited some of those already harboring racial prejudices, allowing them to be much more public with their views. This wasn't a reaction to President Obama's policies but rather was emblematic of the deep-seated racial hatred that parts of America held.

During Obama's presidency, there was also a notable increase in the activities of White supremacist and extremist groups. The Southern Poverty Law Center (SPLC) and the Anti-Defamation League (ADL) both documented surges in the number of hate groups during this period.[18] These groups felt threatened by the rise of a multicultural, progressive America that Obama, in their view, represented. This period also saw the growth of the so-called Patriot movement, including armed militias and groups that advocate against a tyrannical government. Their rapid proliferation during Obama's tenure is no coincidence, as many in these groups viewed his presidency as a sign of impending government overreach.

Finally, beyond overt threats and groups, there was a layer of racialized rhetoric against Obama. Aside from birtherism itself, he was often depicted as "other"—not quite American. Common dog whistles included terms like "Kenyan," "Muslim," or "socialist."[19] These weren't mere political critiques; they were attempts to alienate and de-Americanize the president based on his race and background.

Republican senator John McCain's selection of Sarah Palin as his vice presidential running mate against Barack Obama in the 2008 presidential election served to further debase the Republican Party in terms of what they were willing to accept in future candidates, which led directly to Donald Trump.

Palin's selection was an even more overt celebration of anti-intellectualism than what was seen during the Bush era. Bush often came across as charismatically anti-intellectual in a supposedly "anti-elite" way that appealed to large swaths of America. Palin was different. Rather than an absence of intellectual curiosity, or an indifference to the same, she exhibited a pointed dismissal of rational thought, nuance, and expertise.

By setting this tone, Palin paved the way for Donald Trump, making Trump's brand of aggressive ignorance perfect for his receptive followers. Palin's selection as McCain's running mate conditioned a further segment of the Republican base to not only tolerate but celebrate lack of knowledge and expertise as a badge of honor. Palin served as the final pre-Trump harbinger of the forthcoming "alternative facts" and "post-truth" movement that developed under Trump.

Having been primed by Sarah Palin's vice presidential candidacy in 2008, and further agitated and coalesced by the presidency of Barack Obama, the Republican electorate was ready to accept, and even laud, a leader who didn't just lack knowledge, but aggressively and proudly spurned it.

By the time Donald Trump came down the escalator at Trump Tower in 2015, launching his 2016 Republican presidential candidacy and, ultimately, his general election candidacy in which he defeated Democratic presidential nominee Hillary Clinton, the average Republican voter was ready for him. Trump's disregard for facts, disdain for experts on everything from climate change to trade and foreign policy to the military, and celebration of his gut instincts over experience and nuance might not have worked just a few years earlier.

However, after the Obama presidency, enough Republicans were ready that Trump won the Republican nomination partially through the attrition of other failed candidates, and eventually he won the general election. This became the climax, to date, of the anti-intellectualism and extremism that has been brewing in the American right wing since we started our narrative with the civil rights era in the 1950s.

Trump's rise was the culmination of a series of deliberate choices, proactive strategies, and cultural shifts within the party. Trump's impulsive decision-making, distrust of experts, and embrace of conspiracy theories quickly stood as a testament to how far the pendulum had swung away from evidence-based reasoning and toward ignorance-driven populist rhetoric.

Previous presidents surrounded themselves with experienced experts and advisers, but Trump did not.[20] Often, Trump said he "alone" could fix it. Education was under siege, with vilification of higher learning a commonplace practice in Trump's administration.[21] Trump's abortive handling of the COVID-19 pandemic is at the top of the list of examples,[22] but so are Trump's incompetence in trade, foreign policy, economics, and many other areas.

The mainstreaming of conspiracy theories was one of the most alarming aspects of the Trump era. This ranged from claims about the "deep state" working against him to propagating "Q-Anon" conspiracies,[23] and the end result was a Republican Party that to a great degree gave wild speculation and conspiratorial conjecture the same status as knowledge, reason, and education. This is the post-truth era, where objective facts are less influential in shaping public opinion than appeals to emotion and personal belief. Post-truth paradoxically mirrors aspects of postmodernism, which is particularly ironic given its prevalence among right-wing movements that decry postmodernist thought. Right-wing pundits and politicians, who often claim to champion the pursuit of objective truth and the rejection of relativistic perspectives, have employed post-truth strategies, thereby embracing the very postmodernist principles they claim to oppose.

Trump successfully used populist rhetoric as a tool to supplant policy in appealing to the Republican base. Complex issues were often reduced to sound bites or slogans, which was not a practice unique to Trump, but happened to a degree not previously seen.

In reflecting on MAGA Trumpism, it becomes clear that Trump was neither an aberration for his party nor the originator of ignorance, xenophobia, and racism. Rather, Trump came at the perfect time, with an electorate that had been slowly marinating in those beliefs in private if not always in public. Trump welcomed those views to be espoused publicly, and the debasement and fracture were almost complete.

Now we can supplement our time line with a few other elements to complete our understanding of how American politics broke.

The first element we will add to our time line of radicalization that runs from the mid-1950s through MAGA Trumpism is the Supreme Court. The court, thanks to President Donald Trump's three nominations, became the most right-wing court in decades. Trump's nominations of Neil Gorsuch, Brett Kavanaugh, and Amy Coney Barrett positioned the court to make a number of critical, disastrous decisions that further entrenched the radicalization trends within the Republican Party.

The overturning of *Roe v. Wade* as a direct result of President Trump's appointments looms large in the minds of those concerned since 2016 that a Trump win over Hillary Clinton would lead to exactly that decision. However, Trump's three SCOTUS appointments were significant not just for the decisions made by the court but for the broader cultural message they sent. Not only did they prove that the proudly ignorant can get into positions of power and shape the highest court in the land, but there was much to glean from the way in which these three appointments took place.

Trump's first nominee, Neil Gorsuch, was in a position to be nominated only after Republicans obstructed President Obama's nomination of Merrick Garland to the court in March 2016 because it was "too close to a presidential election." Republicans, led in the Senate by then majority leader Mitch McConnell, ahistorically argued that voters should "have a say" before any nominations were considered, even though President Obama was indeed president until the middle of January 2017.

Proving that this was merely a political strategy and not an actual Republican value, Republicans then gladly and rapidly confirmed Trump's third and final Supreme Court nominee, Amy Coney Barrett, a month and a half before the 2020 presidential election. Barrett was nominated on September 26, 2020, and confirmed on October 26, 2020, mere days before a presidential election. As is the case with many Republican positions, their stated principle becomes irrelevant when it is inconvenient to them.

More broadly, over time the court has been increasingly favorable to business and corporate interests over the rights of individuals. This perception, in part, comes from the *Citizens United v. FEC* decision in 2010 that held that corporations had the right to spend unlimited funds in elections under the First Amendment. In arbitration cases, the Supreme Court has often upheld agreements that compel arbitration and limit class action suits, which some argue benefits corporations over consumers and employees. In environmental law, the court's decisions have sometimes limited the scope of regulations aimed at businesses.[24]

Much more could be said about the Supreme Court and the judiciary more broadly, but suffice it to say for our purposes that it has been an aggravating rather than mitigating factor in the fracturing and breakage that we discuss here.

The final layer to explore comes in two distinct but related pieces: the growth and ubiquity of social media combined with the decline of education.

In the last two decades, but especially since 2012, there has been an unprecedented and historic shift in how people communicate, access information, and form communities. This is a result of the rise of social media platforms, initially like MySpace, Facebook, and the platform formerly known as Twitter, and ultimately including TikTok, Instagram, Snapchat, and others. This has revolutionized our information and social landscape, to some degree in positive ways, and has also altered the political landscape dramatically, contributing to the decline we illustrate here.

By tailoring feeds to an individual's tastes and preferences, social media algorithms frequently build echo chambers and filter bubbles where the content we see aligns with our existing beliefs, interests, past behavior, and preconceived notions.[25] Thus, our beliefs are frequently reinforced and rarely challenged. Over time, this increases polarization, and when one group's beliefs are already radical, it makes them even more radical.

At the same time that we observed social media's rise, we saw the decimation of education. Republicans have gleefully slashed education budgets where they could, especially in already underfunded areas.[26] Where they could not directly slash budgets, they removed topics such as critical thinking, analytical skills, and media literacy from public school curricula. This exacerbates the echo chamber effect described above, and it predisposes students to fall prey to the very breakage we discuss.

The combination of algorithmic echo chambers and diminished skills to think critically and analyze media messages led to the growth of misinformation and disinformation being disseminated and believed. This has had tangible and sometimes violent repercussions. Conspiracy theories such as "Pizzagate" have led to real-world shootings.[27] The general environment created by MAGA Trumpism has led to numerous arrests of would-be shooters and terrorists.[28]

Added to this is the decline of traditional journalism, including newspapers and other media outlets that historically did excellent investigative work. Due to the high cost of investigative journalism compared to the low cost of misinformation and clickbait that spread on propaganda news sites and social media, investigative journalism has been all but destroyed. Instead, sensationalism, bias, and outright conspiracy theories reign supreme on social media.[29]

It's beyond the scope of this chapter, but it bears mentioning that this growth of social media has also had notable mental health implications. Beyond serving as an endless canvas for social and financial comparison, studies on use of social media by young people, including adolescents, are disturbing. Not only is social media a ripe environment for cyberbullying of all kinds; it also encourages aggressive antisocial interactions the likes of which many participants would never dream of mimicking "IRL," in the real world.

None of this should be read as being objectively against social media. If history has taught anything, it is that opposing a new technology and trying to prevent it from existing rarely works. Rather, it adds to the challenges that have been outlined in this chapter.

Each stage of the story we've told offers a piece of how the right wing has chiseled away at the foundational values and common ground that once existed in the United States. The arc from the Civil Rights Movement to the age of social media to the post-truth era has not bent in a positive direction; rather, the trajectory has seen a profound devolution of discourse, understanding, and empathy.

As the fissures deepened, there was less room for nuance, less patience for differing opinions, and an ever-decreasing trust in the institutions that once bound society together. The advent of Reagan's narratives, the manipulation of media by figures like Gingrich, the strategic anti-intellectualism of the Bush era, and the polarizing personas ultimately peaking with Trump each played pivotal roles. External factors such as the unchecked influence of a partisan Supreme Court and the rise of social media in an age of declining educational standards have exacerbated these internal shifts.

Now that we have covered a bit of the time line for how we got to the point of radicalized extremism that represents the American right wing in the twenty-first century, we can move on to the sense of disconnection and disillusionment that leads so many to say "I hate politics," to never get involved in the first place, or to choose to disconnect from the political realm.

CHAPTER 2

WHAT HAPPENED TO CRITICAL THINKING?

In a post-truth world that overflows with information, the ability to discern fact from fiction and to critically evaluate arguments is paramount. Yet as we move further into the twenty-first century, the US faces a paradox. We are more connected than ever, with access to vast amounts of information, but our societal foundations in critical thinking, philosophy, and media literacy are crumbling, to some degree as a direct result of the deliberate attack on these institutions from the American right wing. Part of this is because the Right does not value these institutions.

Another part is because the right wing recognizes the threat that critical thinking and media literacy represent to their espoused worldview and, to the extent that they still have one, their policy platform. The absence of these foundational skills has created a vacuum in our political discourse, allowing misinformation to spread while encouraging and fomenting radical black-and-white thinking on just about every major issue of our time. This chapter delves into the decline of these vital competencies, illustrating the disturbing consequences for our democracy.

It has not always been like this in the United States. Critical thinking has long been recognized for its immense importance in fostering not just intellectually adept individuals but a society capable of nuanced debate, reflection, and informed decision-making. The United States has seen periods where these skills were unanimously held in far higher regard than they are today.

Consider the immense influence of the Age of Enlightenment on the Founding Fathers, or the vigorous debates and philosophical discourses that occurred during the Progressive Era. These eras demonstrate that at various times in our history, deep reflection, logical reasoning, and the ability to decipher complex media narratives were not just appreciated but integral to the nation's progress. As the country navigated the challenges of each era, from crafting its foundational documents to confronting societal change, the importance of these tools in shaping the nation's trajectory was evident.

As is often the case, not every country is suffering in this area as much as the United States. Countries such as Finland or Singapore, for instance, infuse their education systems with strong emphasis on critical thinking and media literacy, aiming to prepare their youth for the complexities of the modern world. The result is that they often boast more informed and engaged citizens, less polarized societies, and an electorate that demands substance over sensationalism from its politicians.

Finland has made multiplatform media literacy and critical thinking a core subject in secondary schools.[1] In math, examples illustrate how easy it is to lie with statistics. In art, image manipulation is demonstrated. In history, historical propaganda campaigns are explored. In language classes, students are taught how language itself can be used to deceive.

Similarly, in Singapore critical thinking skills are taught "in subjects like social studies at the secondary and pre-university levels."[2] In fact, this chapter could be filled with citations from many countries, because the United States is increasingly the outlier in this area.

As we proceed into the heart of the twenty-first century, the American landscape seems to have shifted away from this ideal, and we will explore the importance of these factors to understand their critical role in why the United States finds itself in its current situation.

Critical thinking is the objective analysis and evaluation of issues in order to form a judgment. Simplified even further, it means using facts to generate conclusions. Critical thinking is a discipline of sorts where one evaluates information critically and does not merely accept it at face value. In our context of political discourse, critical thinking allows individuals to evaluate arguments, spot fallacies, and ideally come to an informed decision about policies, candidates, issues, and even the way the discourse itself is carried out. Quite literally, critical thinking in the political system means not simply having a "well-informed citizenry" but maintaining a thriving democracy, or even a democracy at all.

Historically, American education did a far better job than today at cultivating informed and independent thought. It's easy to blame the rise of standardized testing, rote memorization, and ever-dwindling public education budgets for critical thinking's decline, and this would be accurate, but incomplete. The Republican Party agenda and the priorities of the American right wing are also to blame. In the same way that the Right has demonized higher education itself as "liberal indoctrination" for decades, critical thinking itself has been attacked, and rightly so from the standpoint of Republicans. The better able Americans are to think critically and for themselves, the less likely they are to fall for the ideas of the American Right.

For example, the premise of trickle-down economics, that lowering taxes on the rich and reducing government spending will improve economic conditions for members of all economic classes, depends on people being unable or unwilling to think critically. Those armed with basic critical thinking tools would immediately, when presented with such a claim, ask questions such as:

- Do we have historical economic evidence that cutting taxes on the rich helps the economy overall and in particular the lower and middle classes?

The answer is, of course, we do not, because cutting taxes on the rich does not "trickle down" to everyone else.

- Do we have historical economic evidence that when government spending declines, the economy improves?

The answer is, of course, we do not, because government spending—on the right programs—is economically stimulative.

Critical thinking serves as an antidote or vaccine against many bad ideas. However, without the vaccine, the disease enters the body and then must be fought off, which is where we find ourselves today. Without the ability to think critically, people risk becoming passive recipients of information, unable or unwilling to discern truth from lies, vulnerable to manipulation, and lacking the necessary skills to distinguish between conflicting, often nuanced arguments.

The decline in critical thinking has rendered many unable to differentiate between credible sources and misinformation. As a result, political discourse becomes less about the merit of arguments and more about which narrative is the loudest or most sensational. The very fabric of informed democracy is threatened when citizens lack the tools to evaluate information critically.

The last few decades have witnessed a concerted effort from certain segments of the Republican Party to downplay the value of critical thinking. This strategy, whether overt or subtle, serves a dual purpose: it solidifies base support and undermines institutions that traditionally promote critical thought, such as academia. The "liberal indoctrination" narrative not only discredits educational institutions but also paints intellectualism and critical thinking as enemies of so-called traditional values. This anti-intellectual sentiment feeds into a broader narrative where experts such as scientists, economists, or educators are viewed with inherent suspicion. Under MAGA Trumpism, it has become a point of pride not to trust actual experts, instead supporting and trusting a cadre of nonexperts who compete with those bringing actual knowledge of the subject under discussion.

Another strategy has been the promotion of "alternative facts." This concept makes no sense ideologically or linguistically, yet it rose to prominence during the Trump era. Its goal is to establish false equivalence and to create doubt where there should be no uncertainty. For instance, presenting climate change as a "debate" rather than an established scientific consensus on the basis of which varied policy approaches could be considered is a means of immobilizing policy action. By placing unsubstantiated claims on equal footing with empirically supported ones, it becomes increasingly challenging for the public to differentiate between the two, especially without robust critical thinking skills. Corporate media has played a role in this by continuing to stage "debates" between one expert with empirical knowledge on the matter at hand and one lobbyist or professional contrarian armed with nothing more than already-debunked talking points, where each participant is given equal time and placed on equal footing by news outlets.

Our interest being the political system, we find that the dearth of critical thinking in the broader population has had clear repercussions:

ELECTION OUTCOMES

Political campaigns have successfully used misinformation, disinformation, and oversimplified narratives that prey on emotion over logic.

In the 2016 US presidential election, false claims about Democratic presidential candidate Hillary Clinton spread rampantly. One such example was "Pizzagate," a conspiracy theory about high-ranking Democratic Party officials allegedly being involved in human trafficking and a child sex ring, communicating with each other through coded language in emails.[3]

Also thanks to lack of critical thinking, completely unreasonable policy proposals from then-candidate Donald Trump were considered reasonable. Such examples include Trump's promise to build a wall across the entire US-Mexico border, paid for by Mexico, during Trump's first term, or his promise that his son-in-law Jared Kushner would resolve the Israeli-Palestinian conflict during Trump's first term. In reality there are countless examples like these, and a more critically thinking Republican electorate would have realized they were impossible, empty promises made by a candidate, Trump, who likely did not even understand the implausibility himself.

POLICY IMMOBILITY

Important issues such as climate change, health care, and gun control see little meaningful legislative progress because the discourse is mired in partisan bickering, misinformation, and a lack of nuance.

Despite a broad scientific consensus on human-caused climate change, the US withdrew from the Paris Agreement in 2017 under Donald Trump, citing economic disadvantages.[4] The US later rejoined the agreement under President Joe Biden in 2021.[5] A vocal minority questions the veracity of climate science, thereby delaying essential environmental policies. The "Green New Deal" policy framework, which is not the law in the United States as of this writing, has become a source of endless disagreement, including even allegations of socialism from the Right. Aside from the specifics of any of these proposals, the important point is that by generating doubt about the facts, the policy discussion never seriously gets underway and progress stagnates.

CONSPIRACY THEORIES

Unfounded conspiracy theories flourish in post-truth America; whether they concern election fraud, public health measures, or global events, they can be directly attributed to a lack of critical thought. Such theories, once relegated to the fringes, have found mainstream acceptance, leading to mistrust in institutions and even to violence.

In the 2012 presidential election, the "birtherism" about President Barack Obama, discussed earlier, was a conspiratorial storyline. Future president Donald Trump himself pushed this theory in 2011.[6] Although President Obama was easily reelected in 2012, a story without any merit—that Barack Obama was ineligible to be president of the United States and that the story of his birth in Hawaii was a lie—became far more prominent than it should have based on the total lack of factual basis.

During the COVID-19 pandemic, obviously implausible conspiracy theories spread like wildfire, from the Trump administration and also on social media. These include the claims that 5G technology was somehow responsible for the pandemic, that a cure already existed but was being limited only to the rich and elites, that the COVID-19 vaccines that were developed actually were vectors for placing microchips in people's bodies, and many more.[7]

Other conspiracy theories, most deserving no real discussion, also were more widespread than one might think. The belief that Donald Trump would somehow eventually be "reinstated" as president after President Biden's inauguration was popular among many MAGA Trumpists,[8] and of course the belief that Donald Trump was actually the winner of the 2020 election, despite dozens of court cases finding that the claims had no merit and endless explanations debunking the claims, persists even to this day.

Philosophy is sometimes defined as the study of the fundamental nature of knowledge, reality, and existence. Using this definition, its connection to critical thinking within the context of understanding our political breakage becomes clearer. At its essence, philosophy teaches the principles of critical thinking through introspection, logic, ethics, and the questioning of our foundational beliefs. Although distinct from epistemology—the theory of knowledge and investigation of justified belief—the connection for our purposes is significant. Throughout history, philosophical teachings have provided the intellectual backbone for societies to grapple with complex moral and existential questions, even predating the formal definition of critical thinking as a discipline or set of tools.

As with the case of critical thinking, a noticeable erosion in the appreciation for philosophical thought within the general public has led to a more simplistic and unexamined understanding of many pressing issues. Philosophical thought has also suffered as a result of the broad attack on most of the "thinking arts" as mere liberal indoctrination from the American right wing. Philosophy has also provided Republicans the attack line of being a "worthless major" at colleges and universities, which has served the dual purpose of attacking both thought and institutions of higher education at the same time. Republican senator Marco Rubio said in 2015, "We need more welders and less [sic] philosophers."[9]

One of the great gifts of philosophy is that it can provide the tools to dissect and assess moral arguments. Critical thinking can help us answer the question "Is cutting taxes for the rich beneficial to the economy as a whole?" Philosophy, on the other hand, is better equipped to help us consider a different question about taxation, such as "Is it morally justifiable for governments to impose progressively higher tax rates on the wealthy?"

Philosophy as an additional layer on top of critical thinking encourages people to question not just *what* they believe but *why* they believe it. It asks for a deeper introspection that goes beyond surface-level acceptance.

Many pressing political issues, such as the balance between individual freedoms and collective good, are deeply philosophical. Engaging with philosophy helps individuals better navigate these complexities. Unfortunately, as is the case with critical thinking, modern education often sidelines philosophical teachings, sometimes for budgetary reasons, other times for social reasons. More generally, the humanities, including philosophy, are seen as less immediately practical in a job-oriented educational system, a perspective favored by the American right wing.

From a more strictly logistical perspective, a society that increasingly values quick answers and sound bites would naturally push against the slower, more contemplative nature of philosophical exploration, sometimes finding it altogether worthless in answering questions posed by the political system. An all-too-common misconception is that philosophy is an arcane discipline, reserved for ivory-tower academics and not relevant to everyday life, which is absolutely untrue.

As with critical thinking, the right wing has a good reason to oppose teaching students philosophy. Individuals lacking training in philosophical thinking are more likely to consider issues more superficially and to be convinced by simple rather than correct explanations. This heavily favors the offerings of the Republican Party. Consider examples from the right like:

- "Taxes are your money, you worked for it, so you should keep it. Taxes are theft."
- "Fetuses are people, therefore abortion is murder, so all abortions should be illegal."
- "Sometimes immigrants commit crimes, so we should ban immigration."

Such simplistic ideas will take hold much more when targeted at populations lacking in both critical thinking and philosophical thought. The broader societal implications are disheartening.

Without a grounding in philosophy, public discourse becomes shallow, focusing on personalities over principles and, as mentioned earlier, the simplest explanations at the expense of the correct ones. Consider the oversimplified debates on freedom during the COVID-19 pandemic, where mask mandates were framed purely as issues of individual rights without a deeper exploration of communal responsibility and the ethics of care.

Policies crafted without philosophical grounding may lack coherence and long-term vision. For example, the debate around health care often centers on costs without delving into the deeper philosophical question of whether access to health care is a fundamental human right. With climate change, the debate focuses on the superficial, such as whether the government gets to tell you what kind of car you can drive, or what kind of stove you can cook with, at the exclusion of a broader consideration of whether it makes sense to continue putting greenhouse gases into the atmosphere in order to cook our food or drive our cars.

Without shared philosophical principles, or at least a willingness to engage in a serious philosophical debate, societies can become more fragmented, with groups holding extreme positions based on unexamined beliefs, unable to even agree on a basic set of facts.

Thus, in combination with critical thinking, philosophy provides the tools not just to think, but to think deeply and ethically. The erosion of philosophical engagement has led to a shallower, more polarized political landscape and allowed terrible policy ideas to gain public support they do not deserve. Reengaging with philosophy can serve as an antidote, providing depth, clarity, and ethical grounding to public discourse.

Understanding the ideal framework for thinking, let's look at some common examples where the absence of this framework causes material harm to the discourse and becomes an obstacle to solving problems.

GOVERNMENT SPENDING, DEBT, AND DEFICIT

Government spending is a particularly appealing political football for elected officials from both the Democratic and Republican Parties. One side of this debate is that of the debt and deficit, which Republicans endlessly postulate as the key issue when Democrats propose government programs. However, the same Republicans completely ignore debt and deficit when a Republican president presides over massive deficit expansions, such as during the presidencies of George W. Bush and Donald Trump.[10] The other side of this coin is cynically asking "How can we afford that?" when Democrats propose policy and programs, while never asking the same question of military spending, expansion of defense purchases, and fueling the surveillance state under the guise of security.

A political crutch of the Republican Party dating back decades is the appearance of fiscal responsibility as measured specifically through the lens of the national debt and the deficit. This political crutch, a supposedly important value for conservatism, has been used hypocritically, selectively, and with brazen disregard for the truth. When there is a Democratic president in the White House, the Republican Party claims to be shocked and appalled by the increase of the national debt in absolute terms, despite the US having had a national debt for nearly two hundred years. The first layer of deception is talking about the debt in absolute rather than relative terms. The national debt has increased over time, but so has the size of the economy, and the story to be told about the debt relative to gross domestic product (GDP) paints a dramatically different picture than that of the modern Republican Party.

Second, the United States is sadly plagued with a population that is largely ignorant about the difference between debt and deficit. The annual deficit is the government's budget shortfall in a particular year, while the national debt is the total cumulative amount of money borrowed over time. One year of a budget surplus would reduce the cumulative national debt but not eliminate it. The last full year the US had a budget surplus was in 2000 under Bill Clinton, a surplus that diminished in 2001, after George W. Bush replaced Clinton, and was gone by 2002, Bush's first full year in the Oval Office. President Barack Obama reduced the annual budget deficit in numerous consecutive years after replacing Bush, but a reduction in the deficit still increases cumulative debt, or to say it a different way, the country went into debt more slowly under Obama.[11]

These seemingly trivial debt basics, which should be clear even to relatively uninformed individuals, are sources of confusion that can be exploited by those cynically seeking political advantage. Despite regularly claiming that the socially democratic framework proposed by the American Left is untenable, countless global examples of its success exist. George Lakey has explored in his book *Viking Economics*, and during an interview on *The David Pakman Show* in 2016, the clear feasibility of such a system of government.

However, the most egregious way in which the Republican Party weaponizes debt and deficit is by complaining about the deficit when there is a Democratic president but saying nothing when the deficit increases under Republican presidents, which is typical, as seen during the presidencies of George W. Bush and Donald Trump. If pressed and given no opportunity to deny the reality of the data, the typical response will be that the deficit increased under Bush and Trump for unusual and unavoidable reasons, such as George W. Bush's 2003 Iraq War, or Donald Trump's dealing with the COVID-19 pandemic. These claims evaporate under minimal scrutiny, with the understanding that George W. Bush's Iraq War was both optional and a mistake in the sense that Iraq was not the country responsible for the 9/11 attacks, and Donald Trump's deficit increases started long before the COVID-19 pandemic of 2020.[12]

While many Republicans claim to be fiscally conservative without truly caring about the issue, there are plenty of actual fiscal conservatives. However, their hypocrisy comes from supporting, voting for, and often reelecting Republicans who tend to be poorer stewards of the American economy than Democratic presidents. In examining historical budget data, it's quickly apparent that Republican administrations have frequently overseen larger budget deficits as a percentage of GDP than their Democratic counterparts. Republican president Ronald Reagan inherited a deficit of -2.6 percent of GDP from his predecessor, Democratic president Jimmy Carter. By the end of his first term, in 1984, the deficit had swollen to -4.6 percent of GDP. Under Republican president George H. W. Bush, the deficit remained right around this level. Under Democratic president Bill Clinton, there was a notable change. Clinton inherited the deficit of -3.7 percent of GDP from George H. W. Bush. By the end of his two terms, in 2001, the US was running a surplus of +1.2 percent of GDP.

Clinton was followed by Republican president George W. Bush, and the surplus quickly turned into a deficit again. By the end of Bush's first term, in 2004, the deficit stood at -3.4 percent of GDP. It decreased slightly during his second term, but by the time he left office, largely due to the 2008 financial crisis and associated expenditures, the deficit skyrocketed to -9.8 percent of GDP in 2009. Then Democratic president Barack Obama inherited the significant deficit from George W. Bush, and by the end of his two terms, after implementing policies to counter the Great Recession, the deficit had decreased to -3.4 percent of GDP in 2017. More recently, President Donald Trump again reversed the pattern of decreasing deficits under President Obama, already increasing to -4.6 percent of GDP prior to the start of the COVID-19 pandemic.[13]

To be fair, many factors can influence deficits, including global economic conditions, wars, and other crises. However, policies pursued by different administrations, such as tax cuts without equivalent spending cuts (common under recent Republican presidencies) or increased social and infrastructure spending (common under Democratic presidencies), play a significant role in these figures. Nonetheless, there is one party that claims to be a better steward of the economy and to be more concerned with the national debt and deficits, and yet that same party frequently runs higher deficits.

LAW AND ORDER

The "law and order" slogan has been used by Republicans for decades, dating back to the civil rights era. This slogan became an effective way for conservatives to criticize civil rights activists and other progressive movements without directly opposing their aims. Richard Nixon's 1968 presidential campaign prominently featured the law-and-order theme. He presented himself as the candidate who would restore stability and safety to American streets, which he claimed had been overrun by crime and riots. While he didn't openly oppose the Civil Rights Movement, his emphasis on law and order was an indirect critique of the civil unrest associated with the movement and other social protests of the era.

Nixon's first vice president, Spiro Agnew, became known for his harsh criticism of antiwar protesters and civil rights activists, often describing them as threats to social stability and American values. Agnew often framed these groups as lawless and un-American, bolstering the Nixon administration's law-and-order rhetoric.[14]

Ronald Reagan's prominence as a law-and-order figure came later, during his presidential campaign, but during his tenure as the governor of California (1967–75), he took a firm stance against antiwar and civil rights protesters, especially in the context of the protests at the University of California Berkeley. Reagan called for a crackdown on Berkeley protests, asserting the need to restore law and order to the campus and protect the broader public.[15]

Barry Goldwater's 1964 presidential campaign was before the peak of the law-and-order rhetoric, but his conservative stance paved the way for it. While Goldwater was more directly opposed to the Civil Rights Act of 1964, citing concerns about federal overreach, his emphasis on individual liberty and states' rights became foundational to later law-and-order campaigns that indirectly critiqued federal civil rights interventions.

In the more recent political era, the absurd empty promise of adhering to law and order, due process, and the presumption of innocence until one has been proven guilty could not be more stark. There are too many examples to include them all, but some particularly egregious ones will be discussed.

Most notably and horrifically is the January 6, 2021, Trump riots, also known as the attempted insurrection. Despite campaigning in 2020 against lawless protesters associated with Antifa and Black Lives Matter,

and despite fear-mongering about the criminal anarchy that future president Joe Biden would supposedly usher in, President Donald Trump
incited a violent insurrection that included storming the US Capitol on
January 6, 2021, attempting to delay or even prevent the certification of
the 2020 election results that would officially certify Democratic presidential candidate Joe Biden as the president-elect of the United States.
There was rampant criminality inspired by Trump and his associates,
and more than a thousand alleged criminals were arrested and charged
for their roles on that day. Despite the GOP's long-standing position as
the party of law and order, many prominent Republicans downplayed or
excused the violent insurrection. While some condemned the violence,
others blamed Antifa or other groups, despite evidence to the contrary.[16]
Some Republican members of Congress, such as Congresswoman Marjorie Taylor Greene, bemoaned the conditions in pretrial detention for
some of the defendants,[17] an issue that many on the Left have been worried about for decades, which Greene and her ilk only cynically claimed to
care about when it was an opportunity to defend Donald Trump. The contrast between this and their typical law-and-order rhetoric was stark. An
entire book could be written about the Republican reaction to this inci-
dent alone, but to summarize it, there was a complete and total disconnect
from supporting law and order in the reaction of the MAGA right wing.

Throughout his 2016 presidential campaign, Trump and his supporters
repeatedly chanted "lock her up," referring to his opponent, Hillary Clinton, over her use of a private email server. Later, similar chants targeted Joe
Biden. Despite these calls for incarceration, no charges were ever brought
against either individual after extensive investigations. Neither individual
had been indicted, never mind convicted. Calls for their incarceration were
a dangerous departure from law and order and from due process.

In 2023 former president Trump accused General Mark Milley of
committing treason over reported actions he took to ensure military stability in the waning days of the Trump administration. On September 22,
2023, Trump suggested on his social media platform Truth Social that
Milley's treason would be reasonably punishable by death.[18] A comment
further from law and order is difficult to imagine.

While Republicans have been quick to call for punitive measures
against Democrats, there has been relative silence from many in the party
about individuals like disgraced former Republican congressman George

Santos after his indictment.[19] This differential treatment serves as another instance of their selective application of law and order.

Republicans consistently spotlighted Hunter Biden's business dealings and personal life as evidence of the Biden family's alleged corruption and criminality. However, the allegations lacked concrete evidence or were taken out of context, indicating a selective and potentially politically motivated use of law-and-order rhetoric. During the primary phase of former president Donald Trump's 2024 campaign, he regularly promised that he would direct the Department of Justice to imprison and prosecute his political enemies if he were to be elected to a second term in November 2024.[20]

This double standard on law and order also extends into foreign policy. In the immediate aftermath of the 2022 Russian invasion of Ukraine, many of the very same law-and-order Republicans became subtle, and sometimes not so subtle, apologists for Vladimir Putin's illegal invasion of Ukraine. Before the Russian invasion, the GOP often positioned itself as a staunch defender of global order, international laws, and sovereignty of nations. Historically, Republicans have taken a hard line against any breaches of international law. In the wake of Russia's clear violation of Ukraine's sovereignty in 2022, many prominent Republicans did not condemn Russia's actions with the vigor one might expect given their law-and-order stance. Some, rather than unequivocally condemning the invasion, sought to deflect blame or downplay its significance.

Some Republican figures went beyond mere deflection. They appeared to empathize with or even justify Putin's motivations for the invasion, painting him as a strategic genius or a leader simply acting in his nation's best interest. Such apologetics starkly contrasted with the party's typical hard-line stance on violations of international law.

It's worth considering why these Republicans would adopt such a stance. Some analysts suggest that it's due to a combination of oppositional politics (simply opposing the Democratic administration's position) and an alignment with populist elements within the GOP that view Putin favorably. Also relevant is the increased fascination with, sometimes bordering on adulation of, authoritarian strongmen that has surfaced in the Republican Party since Donald Trump's presidency. Trump himself was enamored with Putin, Xi Jinping, Kim Jong Un, Rodrigo Duterte, and other similar leaders.

Analogous to law and order, supporting the troops and being "pro-military" is another typical catchphrase of the right. The swift condemnation of General Mark Milley by certain Republican voices exposed a glaring inconsistency in their "support the troops" mantra. Milley's statement on wanting to understand critical race theory—a mere endorsement of being informed—was met with disproportionate outrage. Suddenly, a decorated and seasoned military official's perspective was deemed irrelevant, even traitorous by some, merely because it didn't align with a certain political narrative.[21]

The military's acknowledgment that climate change is a real and pressing threat to national security would ideally be taken seriously, given the military's primary role in ensuring the nation's safety. Their assessments are based on factual data, strategic considerations, and long-term projections. However, when these assessments collide with the climate change denial narrative, some Republicans dismiss the military's stance altogether. They seem to prioritize ideological dogma over the military's expert analysis on potential security threats.

This double standard is not new. Over the years, whether it was disagreements about strategy in Afghanistan or the military's stance on inclusivity and diversity, whenever the armed forces' perspective deviated from certain Republican viewpoints, their usually unyielding respect for the military took a back seat. However, when those skeptical of interventionist foreign policy raised questions, for example, about the 2003 invasion of Iraq under George W. Bush, not supporting the mission was tantamount to not supporting the troops, according to many of the same Republicans.

THE BUSH ERA AND "UNPATRIOTIC" ACCUSATIONS

Under President George W. Bush, a particularly aggressive brand of patriotism was cultivated, especially in the aftermath of the 9/11 attacks. As the Bush administration set its sights on Iraq, claiming Saddam Hussein possessed weapons of mass destruction (WMDs) and that he was in cahoots with Al Qaeda, opposing the invasion became synonymous with opposing America itself. At this time, patriotism meant going to war, and questioning war meant lack of patriotism.

"You're either with us, or against us," President Bush famously said, setting the tone for what was to come.[22] The now-discredited intelligence used as a pretext for the Iraq War, which claimed that Iraq had WMDs, had severe repercussions for those who dared question it. Opponents were often branded as unpatriotic or even traitors.

At the same time, Senator John Kerry, a decorated Vietnam War veteran and the 2004 Democratic presidential nominee, was a prime example of the emergence of the double standard. Initially, Kerry had voted in favor of granting Bush the authority for military action in Iraq, a position he later revised as the rationale for the war became murkier. However, the Bush campaign was swift to label him a "flip-flopper" for his evolving stance on Iraq. He was attacked for his ultimate opposition to the war, for his criticism of the decision to go to war, and for changing his mind.

THE OBAMA ERA: DAMNED IF YOU DO, DAMNED IF YOU DON'T

President Barack Obama faced criticism from Republicans regardless of his approach to military and foreign affairs. On one hand, his cautious approach to Syria and his policy of strategic patience with North Korea were lambasted as signs of weakness. On the other hand, his aggressive drone strike policy, which targeted and eliminated several high-profile terrorists, was painted as reckless and cruel by the very same Republicans.[23]

When President Obama decided on a military surge in Afghanistan in 2009, critics said it was too little, too late. When he pulled troops out of Iraq, critics said he was abandoning the Middle East. When he intervened in Libya to prevent a potential mass atrocity, he was accused of overreaching and pursuing a policy without a clear endgame. While chastising Obama for not being tough enough on ISIS, many also criticized his decision to strike the terror organization in Syria without specific congressional authorization.

The Republican response was often contradictory because it was not actually based on any principle or set of values, but rather prioritized attacking their political enemies at every opportunity.

THE TRUMP REVERSAL

Donald Trump's position on foreign interventions drastically differed from that of his Republican predecessors. While campaigning in 2016,

Trump declared that he would keep the US out of new wars, suggesting that interventions such as in Iraq were mistakes. He famously said that Hillary Clinton, his then Democratic opponent, would lead the US into "World War III over Syria."[24] Both Trump's stated opposition to military engagements and his attacks on Hillary Clinton for being too hawkish directly contradicted prior Republican rhetoric on military action.

Ultimately, Trump's own foreign policy was unpredictable. He oscillated between praising dictators like Kim Jong Un and threatening "fire and fury" against North Korea. He pulled troops out of Syria, leaving Kurdish allies vulnerable, and also increased troop numbers in the Middle East following tensions with Iran. Most controversially, Trump often contradicted his own military advisors, making abrupt decisions that sometimes caught the Pentagon off guard, like the sudden decision to withdraw from northeastern Syria in 2019. After promising to get the US out of Afghanistan, Trump failed to do so. When President Biden did, Trump attacked Biden for having done it incorrectly.

Hypocrisy, double standards, and inconsistency are glaring markers of a pervasive lack of critical thinking. A robust and rigorous understanding of basic critical thinking concepts instills, at its core, a motivation and capacity to examine the origins of our beliefs. As such, it can serve as a bulwark against falling into inconsistency and double standards. As quickly becomes clear, the only consistency with Republican approaches to the military in the period starting in 2003 is that they will say whatever is most convenient at the time, and whatever allows them to prop themselves up as moral and upstanding defenders of the country while attacking their political opponents. The ever-changing Republican stance on military and foreign policy doesn't just reflect shifting worldviews or geopolitical realities. It underscores a deeply entrenched hypocrisy, wherein the party's foreign policy positions seem grounded less in genuine conviction and more in opportunistic strategies to counteract Democrats.

Another major area where inconsistency is impossible to miss is "family values." Republicans have claimed a monopoly on supposed family values, including Christian values, the family, raising children correctly, and keeping kids safe, despite supporting candidates who live the opposite of these ideals. In reality, these talking points are more about emphasizing heterosexual marriage, the nuclear family, Christian principles, sexual abstinence outside of marriage, opposition to abortion, and an aversion to progressive social values. However, the gap between what they espouse and how many of their representatives act has been notably wide. This disconnect is especially evident in their approach to matters of personal morality, particularly concerning marital fidelity and adherence to the very Christian values they champion.

Despite their claims of upholding traditional family values, many notable Republicans have faced scandals related to infidelity or other personal indiscretions. While personal failings aren't exclusive to any one party, the incongruence lies in the Republicans' strong advocacy for family values juxtaposed with their willingness to overlook these transgressions when politically expedient.

Donald Trump's candidacy and subsequent presidency exemplified this paradox. Revelations about Trump's alleged affairs and hush money payments, illegally disguised as legal fees for which Trump was ultimately found guilty on thirty-four felony counts, and the infamous *Access Hollywood* tape did not deter many self-proclaimed family values Republicans from supporting him. The tacit message was clear: political power and policy alignment can justify overlooking significant moral shortcomings. Despite initially being skeptical of Trump, evangelical Christian Republican primary voters in 2016 ultimately voted for Trump, because their hatred of Hillary Clinton was far greater than their concern about family values.

Donald Trump ultimately saw allegations of sexual misconduct from over a dozen women, including being found civilly liable for sexual assault against E. Jean Carroll in a lawsuit. Alleged affairs, most notably with Stormy Daniels (Stephanie Clifford), a pornographic actress, and subsequent purported hush-money payments didn't deter most of his supporters.

The GOP's alignment with evangelical Christian values is a well-established facet of its identity. However, there are evident contradictions in how these values translate into policy and personal behavior. For instance, while emphasizing Christian charity, compassion, and the teachings of Jesus, many Republican-led policies seem to contradict these very principles. This includes opposition to health care expansion for the needy, policies that separate immigrant families at the border, or a reluctance to accept refugees fleeing persecution who are seeking legal asylum—actions seemingly at odds with the Christian teachings of love, compassion, and sheltering of the oppressed.

In 2023, Republican congresswoman Lauren Boebert was kicked out of a theater for vaping and engaging in sex acts with her date, despite claiming regularly that Democrats are endangering our children through drag shows and supposedly inappropriate school reading materials. Boebert, who is against abortion, became a thirty-six-year-old grandmother in 2023, which she positioned not as a moral failure of any kind but rather as a celebration of life, despite the widely studied inferior outcomes for both young parents and the children of young parents.

Additionally, numerous Republicans who champion Christian values have been involved in scandals that starkly conflict with these teachings, yet they often receive continued support from evangelical bases, revealing a selective application of these principles.

Right-wing political commentator Bill O'Reilly spent years on Fox News attacking urban and Black culture, minorities, and others, but ultimately he was embroiled in a series of sexual harassment allegations and settlements before leaving the network. Former Republican Speaker of the House Newt Gingrich, a staunch advocate of family values, admitted to an extramarital affair while leading the charge against President Bill Clinton over the Monica Lewinsky scandal. Roy Moore, Republican candidate in the 2017 US Senate special election in Alabama, was accused by several women of pursuing them while they were teenagers and he was in his thirties, with some alleging sexual assault. Despite this, he retained the vast majority of Republican support, although he eventually lost the election to Democratic candidate Doug Jones.

An entire chapter could be spent just going over these sorts of examples, but the recurring pattern is the dissonance between public proclamations of moral righteousness, often rooted in family or Christian values, and personal behaviors that starkly contrast with those proclamations.

Critical thinking holds crucial value for a thriving democracy. Critical thinking provides the means to discern fact from fiction, while philosophy encourages the deeper exploration of our values and beliefs.

The processes of erosion of these two facets of understanding are closely intertwined. As philosophical study wanes in our educational system, we find a populace less equipped to wrestle with nuanced ethical and moral questions. This lack of depth and introspection can lead to a weakened capacity for critical thinking. Without the protective barrier of critical thought, society becomes increasingly susceptible to misinformation, especially in an era where media, both genuine and fake, floods our daily lives. The decline in one of these areas inadvertently accelerates the decline in the others, creating a vicious cycle.

Two distinct futures are possible. In one, we continue down our current path, with each new generation increasingly less equipped to think critically, reflect philosophically, or discern media's multifaceted messages. This quickly becomes a race to the bottom, which, with the addition of the newest technologies such as AI deepfakes and voice cloning, will quickly make political discourse even less tenable. Such a world would likely be characterized by even more division, more acute susceptibility to demagoguery, and a troubling ease in abandoning evidence-based decision-making.

We can contrast this with a revitalized society that reembraces these vital disciplines. Here, public discourse flourishes with depth and nuance. People debate the merits of policies based on well-understood principles and evidence, rather than falling prey to emotional or misleading appeals. It's a society that prizes truth, seeks understanding, and fosters a citizenry equipped to grapple with the complex challenges of the modern world. Achieving this second, preferable scenario would depend not only on fixing problems within the educational system but also on addressing social problems, which is difficult to do.

Educators, policymakers, and the public at large must recognize and advocate for the importance of these disciplines. Schools should reintegrate these subjects into curricula, with an emphasis on their real-world applications. Policymakers could support educational initiatives that prioritize these disciplines, ensuring they are accessible to all. For the public, it's vital to demand better and seek out opportunities for self-education and improvement in these areas. Only with collective commitment can we rebuild the foundations of a society that values understanding over ignorance, critical analysis over acceptance, and genuine dialogue over divisive rhetoric.

CHAPTER 3

WHAT ARE FACTS?

Let's start this discussion by taking a look at two very similar but different questions: "What are the facts?" versus "What are facts?"

One type of political disagreement is based around the first question: What are the facts in a particular situation, or about a particular issue? This means understanding the facts about climate change, or infectious disease, or any other issue. Political disagreements could be based solely around what the facts are: substantive disagreements about what policies produce better results or which options for organizing an economy lead to superior outcomes.

Unfortunately, a growing contingent of the American right wing has lost a proper understanding of what types of statements are statements of fact. This leads us to the second question above. Rather than discussing the facts about climate change, the discussion would shift to "What sorts of statements about climate change are facts versus opinions?"

This is an extraordinarily difficult gap to bridge because it prevents the discussion from moving to the substantive stage. When a party to a disagreement falsely believes that the question of whether a vaccine is effective could be a matter of opinion, productive discussion about vaccine policy becomes impossible. When a constituency falsely believes that whether something is against the law is a matter of perspective, productive discourse about criminal justice reform is an impossibility. Before arguing over what the facts are, we must come to an understanding of what types of statements are facts, as opposed to opinions. This is an extraordinarily depressing state of affairs that is responsible for part of the intractability of the political discourse.

A complete understanding of the crisis of fact also requires exploring the role of the Left in this degradation. While most of the criticism falls squarely on the American right wing's total and complete fact denialism, enclaves of the Left have had a role to play through the sometimes-fashionable "my truth" versus "her truth" paradox. Sometimes exaggeratedly described by critics as the "postmodern Left" of "every opinion is equally legitimate," there is no denying that the positioning of truth as subjective by some elements of the Left has caused similar problems to those of the Right's fact denialism and have even allowed the right to co-opt "subjective facts" in a reactionary way.

David W. Angel, a conflict consultant, interestingly writes about the "four types of conversations" in a blog post from December 28, 2016.[1] He categorizes conversations as discourse, dialogue, diatribe, or debate. More relevant to our discussion is his earlier post, "When Arguing Over Value Issues, Sometimes Facts and Truth Don't Matter,"[2] in which Angel explores disagreements over value issues, where the arguments are really over the values that one holds, as well as the often emotional and irrational attachment to those values. This does not make for productive conversation.

Underlying this is the actual lack of ability or willingness to distinguish facts and opinions. A Pew Research Center study released in June 2018 gave participants ten statements, five of which were opinions and five of which were facts, and asked respondents to categorize them. Only 26 percent of respondents correctly categorized all five factual statements as such, and only 35 percent of respondents correctly categorized the five opinion statements as such.[3] These are disturbing numbers.

An example fact in the study was "Spending on Social Security, Medicare, and Medicaid make up the largest portion of the US federal budget." This is an empirical question in that the costs of these programs are knowable facts, and the size of the federal budget is a knowable fact, so this statement is an arithmetic problem of simple division. However, 46 percent of Democrats and 37 percent of Republicans categorized this statement as a statement of opinion.

Conversely, on the opinion statement "Immigrants who are in the US illegally are a very big problem for the country today," 19 percent of

Democrats and a full 50 percent of Republicans said that it is a statement of fact.

An entire category of factual misstatements worthy of exploration covers areas where a president has very little control, and blame or credit are cynically and strategically assigned by Republicans in order to attack an opponent or prop themselves up. Democrats also participate in this to a degree, but in a less consistent and weaponized way. Gas prices and inflation are both examples. High gas prices and high inflation were blamed on President Joe Biden during 2021 and 2022, despite presidents having very little influence over either, and despite the reality that both gas prices and inflation climbed significantly during Donald Trump's presidency before Biden was inaugurated. In fact, if anyone is to be blamed for inflation at all, the supply chain collapse that took place during Trump's failed response to the COVID pandemic would be far more to blame for the eventual increase in inflation than anything President Biden did.[4]

It goes without saying that the lack of distinction between fact and opinion is inextricably linked to our earlier discussions of education and critical thinking. A better educated population would (1) less frequently make statements of opinion as if they were fact in their own discussions, and (2) be less likely to fall for this confusion when elected officials present opinion as fact.

At its core, a *fact* is a statement that can be proven to be true based on objective reality. For instance, "Water boils at 100°C at standard atmospheric pressure" is a factual statement. Its truth can be verified through empirical testing. One's opinion, feeling, or perspective on this fact is irrelevant to its truth. On the other hand, an *opinion* is a belief or judgment that is not founded on proof or certainty. "Chocolate is the best ice cream flavor" is an opinion, as it's based on personal preference and cannot be proven universally true or false.

This would be a natural place to explore logical fallacies, although we won't at this time. As an example, one might wrongly think that if it could be proven that chocolate was the most *popular* flavor, that it might be a "fact" that it is "the best," but in fact, it would still be an opinion, and one would be committing the appeal to popularity fallacy. This would be a fascinating tangent to pursue, but we won't go in that direction.

Historically, societies and cultures have navigated the realm of facts and opinions based on their philosophical foundations, religious beliefs, and sociopolitical contexts. Ancient Greek philosophers like Plato and Aristotle, for instance, spent considerable effort distinguishing between objective truths (facts) and subjective beliefs (opinions).[5] However, during the Middle Ages, religious dogma often held more sway than empirical evidence, leading to some facts being suppressed or rejected if they didn't align with religious beliefs.

With the advent of the Enlightenment and the Scientific Revolution, there was a renewed emphasis on empirical evidence and facts. Yet as societies evolved, the line between fact and opinion began to blur, especially in sociopolitical debates where opinions, backed by selective use of facts or misinformation, often overshadowed objective truths. If the reader feels that this process has accelerated exponentially in the modern post-truth political era of the United States, they would be right.

Human beings are intrinsically driven by emotions, biases, and personal experiences. This makes opinions, which often resonate with personal beliefs or emotions, highly influential. Cognitive biases, such as confirmation bias (where individuals favor information that confirms their preexisting beliefs), play a significant role in this.[6] An opinion that aligns with one's worldview or personal experiences is more likely to be accepted, even if empirical evidence contradicts it.

The digital age, marked by the rise of the Internet and social media, has dramatically reshaped the landscape of information dissemination. While these platforms allow for rapid sharing of knowledge, they also provide fertile ground for opinions to be presented as facts. The echo chambers of social media, where individuals often interact with like-minded peers, amplify and reinforce opinions, making them seem like universally accepted truths. The distinction between fact and opinion becomes further muddled when influential figures or platforms propagate subjective beliefs or misinformation as facts. This has, in particular, fomented the echo chamber as the default environment in which people engage. These echo machines thereby exacerbate the challenge of distinguishing between fact and opinion.[7]

The twenty-four-hour news cycle and the race for clicks and views have led to sensationalism, where dramatic opinions often overshadow nuanced factual reporting. The challenge now is not just finding information but discerning its accuracy and objectivity. From a production and optics perspective, there is a plethora of opinion programming that is packaged as news, for example, much of what is broadcast on Fox News. News consumers have to a great degree been programmed to notice elements on screen that associate what they are seeing with news reporting—reporting of facts. These include but are not limited to the presenters wearing makeup under professional lighting with stylish clothes and a "LIVE" icon at the top of their screen. At the bottom of the screen, the chyron will vaguely describe the topic being discussed in a way that sounds like a "report," such as "climate change debate stirs controversy in Congress." There might be an "on-the-ground reporter" that the anchors cut to, and the name of the program might even include the word "news" in the title.

However, much of this programming is simply opinion programming packaged as news. Sadly, this is very effective. As a reminder about the Pew study earlier mentioned, the results showed that a significant portion of Americans struggled with the distinction between fact and opinion. Only 26 percent of adults correctly identified all five factual statements in that study. Just 35 percent correctly identified all five opinion statements. The study also found that politically savvy, digitally adept individuals were more likely to correctly identify factual and opinion statements. For instance, 44 percent of those with high political awareness (compared to 21 percent with low political awareness) and 36 percent of the digitally savvy (compared to 21 percent who are not digitally savvy) could accurately identify all the factual statements.

Political bias also played a role. For example, Republicans were more likely to classify a factual statement that painted the US in a positive light as "factual," whereas Democrats were more likely to identify it as an "opinion." This is an example of confirmation bias.

The impact of this confusion is significant. When facts and opinions become indistinguishable, the very foundation of rational discourse crumbles. This conflation has profound implications for society, especially in the realms of politics, science, and education. For instance, when policy decisions are based on opinions or misinformation rather than objective facts, it can lead to ineffective or even harmful outcomes. The debate around climate change is a pertinent example, where despite overwhelming scientific evidence, uninformed opinions and vested interests have stalled decisive global action. This inability to distinguish between fact and opinion has had serious political implications in the United States.

The confusion between fact and opinion is far more than a theoretical curiosity or something to consider in the abstract. It is a specific and consequential problem that has become an obstacle not only to political progress, but even to the ability to have sensible and reasonable conversations with friends, family, coworkers, and others in our lives.[8] Although at the individual level, this confusion or conflation can be a less malicious consequence of indifference or ignorance, at the broader political and media level, it's a deliberate tactic employed for political gain. To truly grasp the implications of this phenomenon, we need to understand the reasons behind such strategies and the societal repercussions that ensue.

The first step in exploiting confusion between fact and opinion is creating doubt. By presenting mere opinions as if they were facts while questioning clearly proven facts, the right wing introduces a level of ambiguity into discussions that should in principle be black-and-white. Some statements of opinion might sound like statements of fact, and deliberately confusing them is one tactic. At the same time, some statements of fact can be incorrectly "demoted" to matters of opinion by introducing unfounded doubts.

Echo chambers also contribute to the erosion of societal cohesion and the polarization of public discourse. Individuals within echo chambers are often exposed only to information that aligns with their existing beliefs, leading to a reinforcement of their opinions and a dismissal of opposing viewpoints. This can further entrench ideological divides and make it even more challenging to engage in productive dialogue across political or ideological lines.

On climate change, right-wing echo chambers falsely lead individuals to believe that climate change is a hoax and that no scientific consensus exists. This causes people to dismiss the body of evidence supporting the anthropogenic model of climate change. More importantly, it predisposes those stuck in this echo chamber to reject any serious discussion of what should be done about the problem, since they've dismissed it as a hoax.

With immigration, echo chambers that falsely claim immigrants, both documented and undocumented, commit crimes in the US at higher rates

WHAT ARE FACTS? • 51

than natural-born citizens set the stage to approach the issue from an ideologically extreme perspective, rather than one based in fact.

Echo chambers that reinforce false beliefs about a link between vaccines and autism or baseless supposed "death tolls" from the COVID vaccine lead to groups of people unwilling to even engage in reasonable conversation about vaccines and vaccine policy.

CLIMATE CHANGE

Despite an overwhelming consensus within the scientific community regarding human-induced climate change, right-wing political figures and media outlets have often portrayed this as merely one opinion among many.[9] By framing the discourse this way, they've effectively stalled meaningful action on climate change at various levels of governance.

Another technique has been to pivot the conversation from environmental consequences to economic ones. Assertions like "climate regulations kill jobs" or "renewable energy will harm the economy" are presented as factual, even though many studies indicate that transitioning to a green economy could be a net job creator and have long-term economic benefits.[10] They are also presented, without debate, as if their reality would without question mean that nothing should be done in terms of climate regulations.

COVID-19, VACCINES, AND TREATMENTS

Although peer-reviewed randomized controlled trials did not demonstrate that ivermectin or hydroxychloroquine were effective against COVID, many right-wing media outlets and an army of right-wingers on the Internet insisted that it was either (1) uncertain whether these worked for COVID or (2) a matter of the opinion of doctors whether they worked.[11] Reality was binary: either we had evidence that they were effective for COVID or we did not, and the reality was that we did not.

The development and deployment of COVID-19 vaccines saw a surge of misinformation.[12] Falsehoods covering everything from the vaccines' ingredients to their side effects were touted as facts. Claims that vaccines alter DNA, implant microchips, or cause long-term health issues have all blurred the line between fact and fiction. When purveyors of such disinformation were confronted with the absence of facts and data supporting their claims, they often rested on the idea that these were their truths and their reality.

In certain circles, the seriousness of COVID-19 was frequently downplayed, with comparisons being made to the flu or assertions that only the elderly and immunocompromised were at risk. This opinion, presented as fact, potentially led to complacency in adhering to guidelines and recommendations. Despite the factual reality that COVID was more deadly than the flu, it was considered appropriate by some to have the "belief" (opinion) that it was no more deadly than the flu and therefore no additional precautions were legitimate.

The political objectives behind these strategies are numerous, including:

DIVERT AND DEFLECT

One of the primary benefits of muddling the waters between fact and opinion is the effective diversion and deflection from issues that might be unfavorable or challenging for a political entity. When confronted with uncomfortable truths or allegations, the tactic is not to meet them head-on but to sidestep. By introducing "alternative facts" or casting doubt on established ones, attention is diverted from the original issue.

For instance, consider the Russian interference in the 2016 US presidential election. Instead of addressing the substantive concerns raised by intelligence agencies, the conversation was often deflected to other topics like the "deep state" conspiracies or supposed bias in the agencies themselves. Such deflection mires the conversation in endless debates about peripheral issues, ensuring that the central concern is lost or obscured.

RALLY THE BASE

Manipulating "facthood" serves more than just defensive purposes; it's also an offensive strategy. By challenging widely accepted truths, political entities can appeal to fringe elements and conspiracy theorists, drawing them into the mainstream. This not only broadens their base but also makes it more fervent and passionate.

For the core supporters, this approach reinforces preexisting beliefs. It offers validation, telling them that their alternative views are just as legitimate as established facts. Over time, this emboldens the base, making them more vocal, more active, and more loyal. The rise of QAnon, a conspiracy theory and movement that found significant traction among certain right-wing segments in the US, is a testament to this. Instead of being marginalized, adherents of such theories found themselves validated and emboldened by nods, winks, and occasional endorsements from right-wing political figures.[13]

LEGITIMIZE POLICY DECISIONS

Perhaps the most insidious use of fact manipulation is in the realm of policymaking. When the line between fact and opinion is blurred, it provides a convenient smokescreen behind which controversial or even damaging policies can be legitimized.

Consider environmental regulations. By casting doubt on the scientific consensus around climate change, political entities can justify rolling back environmental protections, framing it as a move to protect businesses from "unfounded" restrictions. Similarly, by portraying immigrants, especially undocumented ones, as inherent threats (a matter of opinion), policies that are harsh or even inhumane can be defended as necessary for national security (a supposed fact).

Furthermore, when critics challenge such policies based on factual grounds, the response is often to dispute the facts themselves. This turns what should be a debate on the merits of a policy into a quagmire about the underlying facts, effectively stalling meaningful critique. This was evident in discussions around the US withdrawal from the Paris Agreement, where the discourse was often hijacked by debates on the veracity of climate change itself rather than the implications of the withdrawal.

Throughout history, societies have grappled with the challenge of discerning facts from opinions. While the tools, platforms, and methods have evolved, the fundamental struggle remains. Understanding this historical interplay provides crucial context to today's post-truth world and informs how we might navigate future debates. From the birth of debate in earlier civilizations, to the Middle Ages' rise of religion pitted against science, through to the Renaissance and Enlightenment, and ultimately landing in the industrial, modern, and postmodern eras, understanding the social, technological, and intellectual landscapes that shaped the progress of debate is critical.

EARLIER CIVILIZATIONS AND THE BIRTH OF DEBATE

The record of the search for truth in the philosophical sense can be traced back at minimum to the Greek philosophers. Socrates's method of elenchus (the Socratic method of eliciting truth by question and answer, especially as used to refute an argument) was about questioning commonly held beliefs, often exposing them as mere opinions rather than facts. One of his students, Plato, continued this tradition, laying the groundwork for empirical study. The Library of Alexandria was a repository of knowledge, and there were undoubtedly debates about which texts held factual accounts versus mere conjectures or opinions. Many ancient Eastern philosophies were built on logic and epistemology, such as in Indian schools of thought including Nyaya, focusing on the means of obtaining correct knowledge.

Even in antiquity, the line between fact and opinion was deeply scrutinized. This arguably led to rich philosophical traditions on which much modern thought is based.

THE MIDDLE AGES: RELIGION VERSUS SCIENCE

In the Middle Ages, the dominance of the church in this tension between fact and opinion was massively relevant. Religious doctrine dictated what was considered a fact. Heliocentrism—the correct belief that the sun is at the center of our solar system—was seen as an opinion, if not outright heresy, compared to the "fact" of geocentrism—the incorrect belief that the earth is at the center of our solar system.

Figures such as Copernicus and Galileo challenged church doctrines with empirical evidence, marking a shift from belief-based "facts" to evidence-based facts. The Middle Ages exemplified the tensions between institutional "facts" and emerging empirical evidence, setting the stage for future scientific revolutions.

THE RENAISSANCE AND ENLIGHTENMENT

The printing press was invented by Johannes Gutenberg around 1440 in Mainz, Germany. It marked a significant advancement in the history of book production and distribution, leading to a massive spread of knowledge and ideas throughout Europe and beyond. The printing press significantly democratized access to information, and it also spread both fact and fiction. As theorist Neil Postman has posited in his book *Technopoly*, the consequences of technologies are in a sense beyond human control.[14] Once introduced, a technology will play out its hand and bring about changes that are not always predictable or controllable. This means that while humans can invent a technology with specific goals in mind, the technology itself will have unintended consequences that go beyond those goals.

In this context, the printing press brought with it the reality of a new environment in which readers must differentiate fact from opinion, and fact from fiction.

Philosophers such as John Locke and Voltaire emphasized reason and empirical evidence. However, they also acknowledged that individual experiences might shape one's understanding of facts. There were also notable debunkings of myths during this time, including, for example, Magellan's circumnavigation of the globe disproving the once "factual" belief in a flat earth.

As human understanding grew, so did our capacity to challenge established "facts" and replace them with more accurate understandings.

INDUSTRIAL AND MODERN AGE

The industrial and modern age saw the rise of newspapers and what we would call the first approximation of modern journalism. This meant greater dissemination of information, as well as the twisting of facts for sensationalism and propaganda purposes. As scientific knowledge expanded at unprecedented rates, debates raged. Darwin's theory of evolution, for instance, was (and still is) contested by some as mere opinion against the "fact" of creationism.[15] During the World Wars, especially World War II, nations manipulated facts to serve nationalistic agendas, muddying the waters between fact and opinion for many.

This age exemplified the potential of information dissemination but also the challenges of misinformation.

THE POSTMODERN ERA

In the mid- to late twentieth century, philosophers like Jacques Derrida questioned the very nature of truth, suggesting that context shapes our understanding of facts. Without judging the value of this movement within the context of critical theory, this perspective, combined with the growing digital age, saw a proliferation of niche sources, leading to echo chambers where opinions were often echoed as facts. Ultimately, fake news and misinformation campaigns, especially evident in recent elections globally, highlighted the growing challenges in distinguishing fact from fiction.

Today, more than ever, understanding the difference between fact and opinion is crucial, as misinformation campaigns have real-world consequences.

While the vast majority of the fact versus opinion confusion has been used by the Right, and it is right-wingers who overwhelmingly fall victims to it, ignoring the elements of the Left in this discussion would leave the reader with an incomplete understanding of this problem.

Historically, left-leaning movements, particularly during periods of social upheaval, have prioritized personal narratives to make their case. From the feminist movements that highlighted individual experiences of discrimination against women to labor movements that recounted workers' tales, the Left used these personal stories to highlight systemic problems. While these accounts were crucial in shedding light on larger issues, they also introduced the complexity of distinguishing overarching truth from personal experience.

Emerging in the mid- to late twentieth century, postmodernist thought, with its skepticism toward metanarratives and emphasis on individual subjectivity, found a resonance within left-leaning circles. The idea that objective truths could be elusive, and individual experiences could hold more authentic insights, gained traction. This resulted in a noticeable shift within leftist academia and politics, where the grand stories of history and society were increasingly viewed through the lens of individual experience.

The term "my truth" has become emblematic of the Left's emphasis on personal narrative. By giving voice to the marginalized and oppressed, it has democratized discourse. However, while empowering, this approach also poses challenges. When everyone's individual truth stands paramount, how does one find common ground or address overarching societal truths? Which "truths" should be given primary consideration when developing strategy and tactics for solving real-world issues?

Coined by Kimberlé Crenshaw, "intersectionality" aimed to understand systemic oppression more holistically.[16] As various identities (race, gender, class) intersect, they can create unique forms of discrimination. This means each individual's experience becomes a valuable testimony to these overlapping injustices. Yet while intersectionality has illuminated many gaps in sociopolitical discussions, it has also added layers of complexity to the fact versus opinion debate.

The Left's focus on subjectivity, while revolutionary, hasn't been without criticism. Detractors argue that an overreliance on personal narratives can sometimes sideline empirical data. For instance, while personal accounts of discrimination are invaluable, they need to be coupled with overarching data to drive policy. Similarly, the Left's approach has occasionally been criticized for potentially creating echo chambers, where only reinforcing narratives are acknowledged, sidelining any contradictory evidence or experience.

A number of examples can be considered here. In the fervor to right the wrongs of the past, there have been calls to remove statues or rename institutions tied to individuals with controversial histories.[17] While the motivations behind these efforts often stem from valid grievances, the discussions can sometimes spiral into subjective territories. For example, judging historical figures by today's moral standards without contextualizing their actions within the time they lived can lead to oversimplifications.

While there are interesting ethical arguments for veganism or vegetarianism based on animal rights, environmentalism, and more, there have been instances where certain activists have made broad health claims that aren't supported by robust scientific evidence. For example, the blanket statement that "meat is unhealthy" lacks nuance and fails to differentiate between processed meats and lean meats or consider portion sizes and overall diet. These opinions are frequently presented as fact, with dissenters attacked.

While acknowledging the real and valid experiences of transgender and nonbinary individuals is crucial, some critics argue that certain activists sometimes oversimplify or misconstrue biological facts to suit a narrative. For instance, stating that "there's no biological difference between males and females" is an oversimplification; while gender is a spectrum and biology is complex, there are certain biological differences between bodies assigned male or female at birth. This becomes immediately evident when considering how an ob-gyn would consider reports of pelvic pain from a biological woman as compared to a trans woman.

While calls for policies such as universal basic income or free college have gained traction among progressive circles, the economic feasibility of these policies sometimes gets entangled in ideological desires rather than hard economic data. The belief that "capitalism is inherently bad" becomes a lens through which all economic policies are viewed, sometimes sidelining nuanced economic analyses. Similarly, while social constructs like race, gender, and class are essential lenses for understanding systemic oppression, there's a danger in making overly broad statements.

The challenge for the Left is to find a middle ground where individual narratives are honored without sidelining empirical evidence. For a holistic understanding of any issue, it's crucial to merge the micro (personal experiences) with the macro (statistical data and overarching facts). Only then can we craft policies that respect individual struggles while addressing larger systemic issues.

Additionally, echo chambers play a role in perpetuating misinformation and reinforcing subjective beliefs as objective truths. Individuals within echo chambers may be more susceptible to accepting opinions as facts, particularly if those opinions are echoed by their peers or prominent figures within their ideological circles.

The journey of the Left, in its approach to truth and subjectivity, offers crucial lessons. While personal narratives bring to light the nuances of systemic issues, empirical truths provide the broader picture. For progressive movements to succeed in the future, these two facets must be considered and appropriately balanced in considering the path forward.

The point here is not to argue that the Left is as culpable in the misguided blurring of fact versus opinion but to realize that the Left is not immune. Unlike the Right, the Left I consider myself a part of still values consistency and seeks to avoid double standards and hypocrisy. As a result, as we criticize the Right along these fact versus opinion lines, we should seek to avoid a double standard.

• • •

WHAT ARE FACTS? • 59

In recent years, the term "post-truth" has evolved from a buzzword into a sobering reality. Living in an era where emotional or biased appeals influence public opinion more than objective facts, the very essence of truth is under threat. To start a path toward a solution, we must unravel the complexities of our current times, tracing the erosion of factuality, exploring its implications, and laying the groundwork for subsequent discussions.

The implications of a society that devalues objective truth are far-reaching and multifaceted. Democracies, which rely on informed citizenries, are particularly vulnerable. Misinformation can distort electoral outcomes, impair public health decisions (as with vaccine hesitancy), and erode interpersonal trust. As falsehoods proliferate, societal cohesion deteriorates, creating fissures that are challenging to bridge.

The media landscape has dramatically shifted with the digital revolution. Traditional gatekeepers of information have given way to decentralized platforms where anyone can be a broadcaster. While this democratizes information, it also allows for the rapid spread of falsehoods. Sensationalism often trumps accuracy in the race for clicks and views. Algorithms on social media platforms inadvertently create echo chambers, reinforcing preexisting beliefs and rarely challenging them. The rise of deepfakes—highly realistic but entirely fake content—further muddies the waters, making it challenging for the average person to discern fact from fiction, never mind fact from opinion.

If misinformation is a disease, education is the vaccine. At the risk of becoming repetitive, a robust educational framework that emphasizes critical thinking, media literacy, and digital awareness is paramount. Schools should focus not just on rote learning but on fostering a questioning attitude. Students should be equipped to evaluate sources, understand biases, and navigate the vast digital information landscape responsibly. Promoting a well-calibrated skepticism—questioning without lapsing into cynicism—is vital.

While education is a proactive approach, legal and regulatory measures are more reactive but equally essential. Laws addressing deliberate misinformation, especially those that endanger public health or security, can serve as deterrents. Regulating social media giants, once thought of as neutral platforms, is a growing area of focus. However, these efforts must strike a delicate balance, safeguarding freedom of expression while preventing the rampant spread of falsehoods.

Misinformation has not only made us question facts but has also further polarized societies. Engaging in productive dialogue requires empathy, patience, and a willingness to listen. It's vital to understand that behind every strongly held belief—that is, opinion—is an emotional core. Building bridges requires addressing these emotional truths, finding common ground, and fostering environments where open, respectful discussions can occur.

The post-truth era presents one of the most significant challenges of the twenty-first century. As the lines between fact and opinion blur, reclaiming the sanctity of truth becomes a collective responsibility. Every individual, community, and institution has a role to play in this endeavor. The journey ahead is arduous but not insurmountable. With concerted efforts across education, regulation, and dialogue, society can navigate its way back to an era where facts are revered and upheld.

CHAPTER 4

THE COST OF PRINCIPLES OVER PROBLEMS

There is a growing trend in right-wing political circles, especially since the Republican Party's wholesale abandonment of policy in lieu of cultural issues, to focus on principles at the expense of solving real-world problems. Understanding one's principles and values, and exploring them in depth, is a good thing. An investigation of one's values and principles can serve as an anchor or guiding light—a foundation on which ideologies, party platforms, and policy priorities can be built. Principles are crucial as they shape beliefs and define identities.

However, the unwavering adherence to principles alone as a substitute for policymaking is one of the ways that the right-wing and often reactionary movements have placed roadblocks to meaningfully addressing problems or proposing solutions to a variety of immediate political, social, and economic questions facing us today. This has become a growing phenomenon within right-wing political circles—a tendency to elevate principles at the expense of addressing the pressing challenges of our time.

This is not merely an intellectual exercise or thought experiment, but rather a predilection with real-world implications. Political entities are frequently rendered ineffective or unresponsive to the very constituents they vow to serve because of endless discussions and debates about principles and values. In addition to exploring the phenomenon itself, we will consider its origins. Why is the gravitational pull of principles so strong? How have social and media realities fueled this trend?

Ideology can distract us from rationality, but it can also distract us from practicality. Those seeking to be effective activists and catalysts for change are well served to understand this tendency, recognize it, and thus be able to circumvent it, pushing for a more productive approach to political discourse—hopefully one of action.

Talking about principles and values endlessly, rather than taking action, can understandably be appealing. The world is undeniably complex. Every day brings with it challenges, ambiguities, and uncertainty. Principles and "our values" can provide a semblance of stability and order—and yet, a singular focus on principles can be a way to metaphorically bury one's head in the sand.

At the heart of principles lies simplicity. They offer easy-to-understand maxims that can appear to be applied uniformly. In the face of intricate problems that require nuanced solutions, principles provide a straightforward lens through which issues can be viewed. This simplicity is often comforting, especially for those overwhelmed by the multifaceted challenges of the modern world.

To be clear, a focus on principles benefits the American right wing. The simple but sadly dysfunctional policy positions that are regularly espoused by the American right wing can only maintain the veneer of plausibility if people divorce themselves from the real world and inhabit the world of theoretical values.

Consider some examples. "A culture of life and non-aggression" often serves as the foundation for decidedly anti-abortion political positions. Focusing solely on this "value," it is easy to ignore the health and rights of the mother, the socioeconomic realities of unplanned pregnancies, and the challenges associated with bringing children into environments where they may not receive the care they need. It also ignores that outright bans on abortion don't actually prevent abortions but rather drive them underground, leading to unsafe procedures that endanger the lives of women.

With taxation, a principles-only approach leaves us in the untenable position of "It's my money, I earned it, so I should get to keep it." This principle underscores a deeply rooted belief in personal entitlement to one's earnings and a resistance to wealth redistribution through taxation.

The difficulty is in actually applying this view to public policy and living in a society. Such a "principled" view leads to resistance against progressive taxation, where the wealthy are taxed at higher rates, or even against any taxation at all. However, a society functions with a collective contribution. Taxes are used to build roads, schools, hospitals, and other public infrastructures from which everyone benefits. Taxes fund social safety nets that help stabilize society, ensuring that the less fortunate are not left in dire conditions, which in turn benefits the entire community by reducing crime, poverty, and public health crises. By focusing solely on the principle of individual entitlement to wealth, one can overlook the broader benefits that come from a collective financial responsibility in maintaining a functional and harmonious society.

Principles also play a pivotal role in generating our identities. They demarcate boundaries, creating a clear distinction between "us" and "them." By aligning with certain principles, individuals signal their affiliations, cementing their place within a particular group or ideology. This sense of belonging is vital, fulfilling a fundamental human need for connection and validation, but it completely ignores the policy questions and practical realities of living in a society with others.

Adherence to principles often comes with a perceived moral superiority. By prioritizing principles above all else, individuals can position themselves on a higher ethical plane, asserting the righteousness of their stance. This moral certitude can be empowering, allowing individuals to advocate for their beliefs with unwavering confidence. However, its impracticality quickly surfaces.

A stated value often repeated in the context of the COVID-19 pandemic was "Parents should have the sole right to decide how to raise their children." This was applied to questions of masks and vaccines, but also to curricula in school, including lists of assigned books. It emphasized the rights of parents over the expertise of both medical experts and teachers.

This principle quickly clashes with the rights and welfare of children, and also with the ability of schools to maintain an ideal learning environment for children. While parents might cite personal or religious beliefs to decline medical treatment for their children, doing so in cases of life-threatening illnesses can lead to unnecessary suffering or death, as seen in cases where parents refuse blood transfusions or cancer treatments for their children. Additionally, allowing parents full autonomy might also inadvertently provide cover for abusive practices. Balancing parental rights with the child's rights and well-being demonstrates the complexity and nuance required beyond the initial principle. In a practical sense, the "principles" crowd also has no temerity about placing their opinions above the expertise of medical experts and teachers.

One can insist that they are "against foreign military intervention," but strict adherence to such a principle becomes problematic when atrocities like genocide, ethnic cleansing, and severe human rights abuses occur. A tension between nonintervention and a responsibility to fellow humans quickly arises. A dogmatic adherence to nonintervention for its own sake can allow massive human rights abuses to go unaddressed and unchallenged.

Another appeal of principles is that by their nature, they are steadfast and can be completely unchanging. Their predictability and (often) simplicity are enticing, especially in a volatile world. Much like conspiracy theories for the conspiracy theorist, focusing on abstract principles alone can provide a security blanket, insulating one from having to make genuinely difficult decisions based on what is presently taking place in the real world. This conflict between principles and practiwcality is understandably difficult for many.

Grappling with conflicting ideas or beliefs can be mentally taxing. Principles offer an escape from this cognitive dissonance. By adhering strictly—or appearing to adhere—to a set of core beliefs, individuals can conveniently sidestep the discomfort of contradictory information or perspectives. The allure of principles is undeniable, but their overemphasis can prove detrimental, especially when they overshadow pressing problems.

The American right wing has historically benefited from a focus on principles over policy in large part because of the stark contrast with the Left's approach. The Left, with its orientation toward equity, justice, and inclusivity, often grapples with the inherent complexities of these ideals. These worthwhile progressive ambitions involve layers of nuance and intricacy, recognizing that a one-size-fits-all approach and black-and-white thinking are not adequate to address real-world disparities and systemic issues.

The Right's focus, on the other hand, is on broad, overarching principles, like "individual liberty" or "states' rights." This allows for a simplification of the narrative beyond what is reasonable. This simplicity is enticing, as it presents issues as attractive black-and-white questions, creating a clear distinction between "us" and "them" and relegating nuanced debate to the dustbin. If issues are this simple, why would one need more lengthy debate or discussion? This binary approach is more palatable for many and plays well in sound bite–driven media environments. It's an effective rhetorical strategy, especially in polarized climates, as it can rally a base around a shared, clearly articulated belief, regardless of the complexities of the issues at hand.

This "principles-first" approach also provides the Right with a shield against criticism. By framing their positions as steadfast adherence to deeply held values, they can portray policy challenges as ideological attacks and appear to take the consistent moral high ground. This obviates critiques based on evidence or outcomes and allows the circumvention of criticism altogether. Nuanced debate is dismissed and the Left's engagement with intricate policy details ends up portrayed as a mere distraction from these "core" principles. Ultimately, substantive policy discussions are sidelined and meaningful societal progress is halted.

Historically, the American right wing has invoked principles, often in tandem with a perceived moral high ground, to stymie progressive initiatives, create ambiguity around clear-cut issues, and shift the discourse away from evidence-based policy discussions. A number of instructive examples are available for consideration.

THE CIVIL RIGHTS MOVEMENT AND THE CIVIL WAR: "STATES' RIGHTS"

In the 1950s and 1960s, as the Civil Rights Movement gained momentum, demanding equal rights for Black Americans, many conservative politicians and groups opposed these changes by championing the principle of "states' rights."[1,2] They argued that individual states should have the autonomy to determine their own policies on segregation and voting rights, a tactic used to maintain the racially segregated status quo in the southern states.

A myopic focus on this principle of "states' rights" at the exclusion of a discussion based on the substance of what states wanted to do with those rights became prevalent. This is not dissimilar from the states' rights invocations during the Civil War, where "states' rights" were invoked to avoid dealing with the wrongness of slavery. Of course, it was not merely about "states' rights" but more specifically "states' rights to keep slavery legal."

CLIMATE CHANGE: "ECONOMIC FREEDOM"

Recognizing the threat posed by legislation aimed at curbing carbon emissions to certain industries, the right wing, often backed by fossil fuel interests, has presented the fight against climate change regulations as a battle for "economic freedom" and against government overreach. Often, "small government" will be invoked. This framing clouds the debate around clear scientific evidence of anthropogenic climate change and the urgency of the issue, stalling significant policy measures.

It is true that at the heart of the climate change debate is the tension between economic growth and environmental responsibility. The right wing, particularly in the United States, has frequently framed climate regulations as threats to jobs, industries, and the broader economy.[3] By honing in on the principle of "economic freedom," they pivot the conversation away from the overwhelming scientific consensus on human-caused climate change and actionable policy discussions. Instead, the narrative becomes one of overbearing government intervention versus the rights of industries and workers. This perspective conveniently overlooks the long-term economic costs of environmental degradation and the potential economic benefits of transitioning to cleaner energy sources.

It warrants a mention that another common tactic is to challenge the very science of climate change. While a vast majority of climate scientists agree on the anthropogenic causes of global warming, the right has managed to create a sense of debate by elevating a few dissenting voices.[4] The principle invoked here is one of "intellectual diversity" or "academic freedom." By arguing that all viewpoints, regardless of their scientific validity, deserve equal weight in the debate, they effectively stall legislative actions, portraying them as premature or overly reactionary.

GUN CONTROL: "SECOND-AMENDMENT RIGHTS"

At the heart of the gun control debate in the United States is the Second Amendment. The right wing, with considerable backing from organizations like the National Rifle Association (NRA), has often presented this amendment as sacrosanct, an unassailable right that cannot and should not be curtailed in any form. The mechanisms for obtaining firearms in the United States have become inextricably linked with an intractable conflict between individual rights and public safety. A "principles-only" approach to gun safety often is used to suggest that any restrictions on gun ownership equate to an erosion of fundamental freedoms.

To counter calls for stricter gun regulations in the aftermath of mass shootings, a narrative has been popularized: "The only thing that stops a bad guy with a gun is a good guy with a gun."[5] This principle of self-defense and individual heroism sidelines statistics showing that countries with stricter gun laws tend to have far fewer gun-related deaths.[6] It also minimizes data indicating that increased gun ownership can lead to more household accidents and escalations in domestic disputes.[7]

Another tactic employed to prevent gun regulation is the slippery slope argument. The principle here is that any regulation, no matter how minor or reasonable, sets a precedent that will eventually lead to the total confiscation of firearms and the unconstitutional curtailment of Second Amendment rights. By instilling this fear, the right wing can rally opposition against even the most basic measures, such as universal background checks or restrictions on bump stocks, portraying them as the first step in an inexorable march toward tyranny.

HEALTH CARE: "INDIVIDUAL LIBERTY"

The American health-care debate epitomizes how principles can overshadow practical considerations. At the crux of many conservative arguments was the notion that health-care decisions should be a matter of personal choice, free from governmental intervention. This perspective sees health care not as a right but as a product, one that individuals should purchase according to their means and needs, subject to the same market conditions and forces as mobile phones or basketball sneakers.

The most recent major reform to health care and health insurance in the United States was the Affordable Care Act (ACA), known as Obamacare. A central tenet of the ACA was the "individual mandate," which required all Americans to have health insurance or pay a fine. While this was designed to ensure a broader, healthier pool of insured people and thus stabilize insurance markets, it was met with considerable opposition from the Right. Critics argued that it was an overreach of governmental powers, forcing individuals into the insurance market against their will, infringing on the principle of individual liberty by forcing them to engage in commerce.[8]

Another narrative that emerged was the perceived economic burden of the ACA. Principles of free-market economics were evoked to argue against government "interference" in the health-care industry. Concerns were raised about potential job losses, increased taxes, and the sustainability of such a system, despite evidence from other developed nations demonstrating the feasibility and benefits of universal or near-universal coverage.[9,10]

While much attention from conservatives was focused on the potential negative consequences of the ACA, less emphasis was given to its tangible benefits. By protecting those with preexisting conditions, allowing young adults to stay on their parents' insurance until age twenty-six, and expanding Medicaid in participating states, millions gained coverage. Yet these benefits were often downplayed or ignored in favor of arguments centered around principles of personal freedom and economic liberty.

Another principles-based angle in this debate was the moral principle that individuals should be responsible for their health outcomes and, consequently, their medical bills.[11] This viewpoint often neglects the systemic issues at play, such as the exorbitant costs of medical procedures and medications and the inaccessibility of preventive care for many, framing health-care accessibility as a result of personal merit rather than a societal obligation—never mind environmental issues such as the cigarette smoke of others, pollution from fossil fuel companies, and so many other externalities that go beyond one's personal choices.

By repeatedly placing principles over tangible policy outcomes, the right wing in America has historically succeeded in stalling or reversing progressive initiatives. Republican senator Rand Paul, for example, stuck a wedge into the wheels of progress toward universal health care by likening it to slavery in principle. On May 11, 2011, Senator Paul said:

> With regard to the idea of whether you have a right to health care, you have to realize what that implies. It's not an abstraction. I'm a physician. That means you have a right to come to my house and conscript me. It means you believe in slavery. It means that you're going to enslave not only me, but the janitor at my hospital, the person who cleans my office, the assistants who work in my office, the nurses. Basically, once you imply a belief in a right to someone's services, do you have a right to plumbing? Do you have a right to water? Do you have [a] right to food? You're basically saying you believe in slavery.[12]

This strategy, while effective in the short term for political gains, often leads to a neglect of pressing issues and the undermining of democratic processes that thrive on informed debate and consensus-building.

It should not be ignored that there is also a media environment reality that has significantly fomented endless theoretical debates about principles at the exclusion of solving real problems and making progress on policy. The current media infrastructure, driven by financial motives and the hunger for attention, profits more from prolonged, principles-based debates than concise policy discussions. This is even more significant and pronounced in the alternative and online media space that has taken a turn toward long-form content over recent years, culminating in the status quo of content creators regularly publishing episodes that are three, four, or even five hours in duration.[13]

In the digital age, attention is currency, metaphorically and literally. The more clicks, views, and engagement a topic garners, the more profitable it becomes. In some cases, the link is direct and overt, such as higher rates of monetization based on longer "watch time" metrics. Media corporations and individual creators alike have recognized and leveraged this model to their advantage. In the vast landscape of modern media, there's a conspicuous trend: content that is polarizing, controversial, or dives deeply into abstract principles tends to gain more traction than straightforward, policy-based discussions. From this, the two-, three-, four-hour and sometimes even longer podcasts, debates, and discussions have surged in popularity. In the alternative media ecosystem that I inhabit, longer videos, episodes, and streams translate directly to higher watch time metrics and thus more revenue.[14]

One reason is that principles-based debates are inherently open-ended. They offer a platform for endless back-and-forth arguments, each side often entrenched in its position, leading to hours of discussion that can be segmented, dissected, and spread across various episodes or articles. This model perfectly fits both the continuous corporate media news cycle, where the aim is to keep the audience hooked, returning for updates, and engaging in the comments or on social media, and the independent online media space. In this setup, a debate on "freedom versus regulation" will always outlive a discussion on "specific provisions of a health care policy."

As media has moved increasingly online, the metrics of success have shifted. It's no longer just about the breadth of viewership but the depth of engagement. Long, drawn-out debates, especially those that elicit emotional reactions, ensure viewers or readers stay engaged longer, leading to higher ad impressions and increased profitability. Think of the numerous YouTube channels, podcasts, or blogs that delve deeply into philosophical quandaries or principles-based arguments. They build dedicated communities around these debates, which often sprawl out over hours and multiple episodes. It's a win-win for content creators and platforms alike: creators build loyal audiences, and platforms benefit from prolonged user engagement.

In many ways this is a welcome change from the four-minute "debates" hosted by corporate media on issues as complex as climate change. However, there's another side as well. These debates and conversations often result in a public that is more divided, less informed about actionable policies, and more likely to be stuck in echo chambers. The essential task of media—to inform and educate its audience—gets overshadowed by the profit-driven motive to entertain and engage. The outcome is a citizenry that's well-versed in debating abstract principles but often ill-equipped to navigate the nuances of real-world policy or the implications of legislative decisions. In this tug-of-war between profitability and informative value, it's crucial to ask: At what cost does this diversion come to our democracy?

I've dealt with this head-on during live call segments on my program where viewers and listeners seek to engage with me on questions such as:

- "What are your ethical principles?"
- "Where do you stand on the coerciveness of government?"
- "How do you define truth in the modern age?"
- "How do you reconcile personal liberty with societal order?"

All of these questions are intriguing and valuable and can open the door to hours of philosophical discussion. However, they also will rarely lead to concrete solutions or a clear understanding of policy implications. The question then becomes, what is our goal in engaging with these questions at all?

As a podcaster and YouTuber, I aim to create content that informs and educates, while being entertaining enough to draw and keep an audience, all oriented at highlighting particular issues and stimulating action—ideally action that moves society in a decidedly positive direction. Without considering our principles and values, it is impossible to even start this process. Nonetheless, to avoid getting lost in the principles, a balanced approach is necessary. The guiding and overarching principle in finding this balance between values and pragmatism is ultimately knowing and understanding the end goal of our engagement, whether it's as a podcaster or YouTuber, or simply as someone engaging with family around the dinner table about the local issues of the day.

Due to their abstract and open-ended nature, a principles-only focus leads to long-winded discussions without arriving at any concrete conclusions. Since my goal is to arrive at concrete conclusions, it's important to know when to move from principles to specifics. Sometimes, a philosophical black hole can open up, where ideas and principles disconnect from real-world issues and solutions. If a creator's aim is to address contemporary problems or propose actionable solutions, then getting sidetracked by these philosophical questions leads away from that goal.

Another risk is that wading into philosophical waters can quickly lead to the oversimplification of issues, falsely making them appear to be about some simple theoretical black-and-white choice, such as individual freedom versus societal good, which just so happens to also benefit the American right wing. Taking the position that government intervention is inherently bad, as a principle, and thus should be limited, leads to disastrous policy conclusions, including the rejection of government involvement in definitively useful areas, such as preventing monopolies, ensuring basic public safety, and others.

Adherence in the abstract to the principle that "people should be self-reliant" can lead to policy conclusions that would eliminate the possibility of a social safety net, exacerbating social inequalities, among other adverse outcomes. The belief that "free market solutions are always best" can lead to the inaccessibility of health care or other basic public goods.

Engaging in these abstract discussions can sometimes create a disconnect from real-world issues and solutions. If a creator's aim is to address contemporary problems or propose actionable solutions, then getting sidetracked by these philosophical questions can detract from that goal.

The bottom line is that in today's political and media climate, the allure of abstract principles is both evident and tempting. Principles can serve as a beacon, guiding our beliefs and shaping our identities and priorities. On the other hand, unchallenged adherence to principles, especially at the expense of pragmatic solutions to real-world challenges, is detrimental. We've highlighted the nuances of this trend, with a particular focus on the American right wing's predilection for prioritizing principles over policy.

The media landscape of our era exacerbates this trend. While deep dives into abstract principles might be good for engagement metrics, they often divert from actionable solutions and policy-focused dialogues. For any movement, party, or ideology to be truly effective, it must strike a balance between its foundational principles and the pragmatic realities of governance and societal progress. Focusing solely on principles, especially to the exclusion of actionable solutions, can lead to gridlock, confusion, and ultimately stagnation. The challenges of our era—such as climate change, systemic inequalities, or public health crises—require nuanced, evidence-based solutions, not just philosophical stances.

For those on the front lines of the media, like podcasters, YouTubers, and writers, the responsibility is twofold: to engage in and promote meaningful discussions that are rooted in principles but also to pivot toward pragmatic solutions. These conversations should serve as a starting point, a means to an end, rather than an end in themselves.

Ultimately, there is an attractive but false notion that to be valid and worthy of being listened to, one must (1) have defined every principle and value they subscribe to and (2) apply those principles unwaveringly and perfectly in every real-world situation. The truth is that the real world is complex and messy. The principle I apply to "individual freedom" might be different when it comes to choosing our careers and professions than it might be when considering vaccination requirements to attend public school, or the responsibility to pay taxes in order to live in a modern society with public goods that we can all count on. Principles and values can be applied judiciously by evaluating real-life situations on a case-by-case basis. This is a feature of being human, not a bug.

CHAPTER 5

WHY CHOOSE LEFTISM?

We now detour from examining the historical forces that led to this fracturing of national unity and decline of critical thinking and pivot to the story of successes and repairs. This is not merely an academic exercise but a deliberate effort to draw lessons from the past that can inform the ideal path forward. By examining these movements, we can uncover the strategies, values, and actions that have worked to mobilize communities, influence politics, and foster more functional societies.

A detailed look at successful left-wing movements serves a dual purpose. First, it provides reason for hope, and a reminder that change is not only possible but has been achieved in a variety of circumstances, many quite challenging. These movements varied in scope and scale across times and geographies and offer insights into how ideologies centered around justice, equality, and solidarity can translate directly into tangible, measurable progress.

Second, this focus acts as a guide and frame for the discussions to follow, emphasizing that the principles and tactics of these movements aren't mere relics of the past but actionable tools for today and tomorrow. It underlines the importance of learning from history to avoid the pitfalls of repeating it, with the ultimate goal of crafting a future that aligns more closely with progressive ideals.

A popular refrain from the right wing is that "leftism simply does not work." Often, the Soviet Union, Cuba, or Venezuela will be cited as examples. These are poor examples of the successes of leftism insofar as they are not leftist countries in the style of social democracy but rather authoritarian regimes led by strongmen dictators and wannabe dictators.

Before we look further at how we can confront the dangerous assault on critical thinking from the Right, it's important to consider the true successes of leftism and why it presents values and democratic solutions worth fighting for. We will not consider every example of success, but it's useful to look at some cases and places where leftist popular movements have succeeded with broad benefit.

Across the globe, numerous countries, states, and municipalities have seen left-wing governments or movements produce tangible, positive results. These countries and regions usually have many of the hallmarks of social democracy, including low corruption, high standards of living, and thriving business environments.

The subject matter of this chapter is resisted heavily by those who simply do not want to admit that this kind of thinking can bring success. When one presents the modern American right wing with examples outlined in this chapter, some claim that there was no actual success, and if there was, it was thanks to elements of the government that were not actually left wing. For this reason, we start by defining leftism.

At the heart of any debate or discussion is a fundamental necessity: clear definitions. Without a mutual understanding of the terms being employed, debates can quickly devolve into people talking past one another. So let's clarify what we mean by "leftism" in this context.

SOCIAL DEMOCRACY

The term "social democracy" evolved over the twentieth century, particularly in western Europe, into a form of well-regulated capitalism that has decided to socialize—in other words, to remove from the whims of supply, demand, and markets—some aspects of the economy and society. It does not advocate for the elimination of capitalism, but rather is a form of capitalism that harnesses its productive capabilities while ensuring that its excesses are moderated. Key features of social democracy include:

• Market economy: Unlike socialism, which often seeks to socialize ownership of major industries to all workers or even to the state,

social democracy acknowledges the efficiency and innovation that
can arise from a competitive market environment.
- Regulation: While markets are allowed to operate, they are not
left unchecked. Regulations are put in place to prevent monopolies, protect consumers, safeguard the environment, and more.
- Welfare state: One of the hallmarks of social democracy is a robust
welfare state. This includes programs and initiatives like universal
health care, free or subsidized higher education, and strong unemployment benefits.
- Redistribution: Through progressive taxation and other measures,
social democracies aim to reduce vast income and wealth inequalities. Higher taxes on the wealthiest are used to ensure that no
one's standard of living falls below a certain level.

It is essential to understand that both socialism and social democracy
aim for social justice and a reduction in income inequality. However, their
methodologies differ, with social democracy working within a capitalist
framework. Mistaking social democracy for socialism is a common error,
often propagated by those who either misunderstand the terms or, at
times, deliberately misrepresent them for political reasons.

In this context, for our evaluation, when referring to leftism, we are
talking about social democracy. It's a vision of society where markets and
compassion coexist, where businesses can thrive, but not at the expense of
the broader public welfare. This form of governance has been successfully
implemented in various nations, leading to some of the highest standards
of living globally. As we proceed, we'll explore how this blend of regulated
capitalism has not only worked but thrived.

One of the most significant and most frequently cited models for social
democracy is the Scandinavian countries of Denmark, Norway, and Sweden. Finland is sometimes included in this group, although it is not part
of Scandinavia. Indeed, these serve as compelling examples of how social
democracy can lead to prosperous, stable, and equitable societies. The addition of Iceland to the conversation, although less common, rounds out a
list of the five Nordic countries.

Historically, the Nordic model evolved from a combination of free-
market capitalism and a comprehensive welfare state. After World War

II, these countries made a deliberate move toward social democracy, recognizing that a balance between market forces and state intervention was crucial for societal well-being. Consistently, the Scandinavian nations rank high on global indices measuring quality of life, happiness, and human development.[1] A combination of efficient public services, robust education systems, and a focus on public well-being has led to citizens enjoying a high standard of living.

Transparency International's Corruption Perceptions Index often ranks these countries among the least corrupt in the world.[2] A culture of trust, strong institutions, and stringent regulations help ensure that public and private sectors operate with integrity. While no country is entirely free of crime, Scandinavian countries tend to have low crime rates, particularly violent crime.[3] This can be attributed to their focus on rehabilitation rather than punishment, comprehensive social safety nets, and educational opportunities that reduce economic disparities.[4]

Contrary to some right-wing misconceptions, these nations are not anti-business. In fact, they have thriving entrepreneurial ecosystems that have created global giants such as IKEA, Volvo, Nokia, and Spotify. Their approach is not to stifle business but to ensure that business growth does not come at the expense of workers' rights or the environment.

In fact, according to the World Bank's "Doing Business" reports, Denmark, Norway, and Sweden consistently rank among the top nations for ease of doing business.[5] These rankings take into account factors such as starting a business, dealing with construction permits, getting electricity, registering property, getting credit, protecting minority investors, paying taxes, trading across borders, enforcing contracts, and resolving insolvency.

The World Economic Forum's Global Competitiveness Report, which assesses factors such as infrastructure, macroeconomic stability, health, education, and the business environment, consistently ranks Nordic countries in its top tiers. For instance, in recent reports, Finland has been lauded for its innovation capability, while Sweden has been noted for its vibrant business dynamism.[6]

Particularly in cities such as Stockholm and Copenhagen, the start-up ecosystems have been thriving. Stockholm, for instance, has been dubbed the "start-up capital of Europe," producing a significant number of "unicorns" (start-ups valued at over $1 billion) per capita, second only to Silicon Valley.[7]

Perhaps the most defining feature of these nations is their expansive welfare systems. From universal health care to free higher education, from generous parental leave policies to unemployment benefits, the Nordic model ensures that while individuals are free to pursue their ambitions, they are never left destitute or without support.

In essence, the Scandinavian social democracies provide a blueprint for how nations can achieve prosperity while ensuring that the fruits of this prosperity are shared more equitably among their citizens. They showcase that left-wing governance, when implemented judiciously and tailored to a nation's unique context, can lead to outcomes that benefit the vast majority of the populace.

Let's now consider two common attempts by the Right to contradict the claims about social democracy's successes. The first is that it is the most capitalistic, right-wing elements of these societies that are responsible for their success. The second is that it is only because these countries are homogeneous and racially White that they have succeeded. We will consider each argument in turn.

THE SCANDINAVIAN/NORDIC CAPITALISM MYTH

A recurring argument posited by some critics is that the success witnessed in the Nordic countries is solely a result of their capitalistic elements, with social democracy being a mere weight pulling them down. This perspective is an oversimplification and fails to recognize the harmonious synergy these nations have achieved between capitalism and social welfare.

A key feature of the Nordic model is the emphasis on workers' rights and welfare. This isn't just altruistic; there's a strong economic rationale behind it. Happier, healthier workers are more productive.[8] In turn, higher productivity enhances economic performance. A balance between work and leisure, ensured by shorter work weeks and ample vacation time, leads to rejuvenated workers who contribute more efficiently when they are at work.

The social democratic emphasis on accessible and high-quality education results in a highly skilled workforce.[9] With more individuals having access to higher education, these countries benefit from a talent pool that's diverse and well equipped to tackle modern challenges. This is a direct result of social investment, not pure capitalism.

The safety nets in Nordic countries encourage entrepreneurship. Knowing that risks such as health crises won't lead to personal financial ruin can embolden individuals to start businesses. This has been observed in Denmark, where a strong safety net has led to high entrepreneurial activity.[10]

While Nordic countries have thriving private sectors, they also have significant public ownership in key sectors, ensuring that essential services remain accessible to all and are not solely profit-driven. This is a distinctly social democratic feature and contributes to both societal welfare and economic stability.

It's a mischaracterization to credit only the capitalistic elements for the success of the Nordic model. The social democratic components don't just coexist with capitalism—they enhance and shape it to produce societies that are both prosperous and equitable.

SOCIAL DEMOCRACY'S SUCCESSES

A frequent criticism or explanation posited by detractors of social democracy is that Scandinavian success is attributable to their racial and cultural homogeneity. The idea suggests that these countries' societal achievements are due to a lack of ethnic diversity, implying that diverse nations cannot replicate their success. This viewpoint is simplistic and flawed for several reasons.

Even before the recent waves of immigration, these countries had their share of regional, linguistic, and cultural differences. For instance, Finland has a significant Swedish-speaking minority, and Norway had historical divisions between its coastal and inland populations.

Moreover, in recent decades, countries like Sweden and Norway have taken in a significant number of immigrants. As of recent data, approximately 19 percent of Sweden's population and 17 percent of Norway's were born abroad.[11] These nations have faced challenges integrating immigrants, as any nation would, but they continue to maintain their high standards of living and social cohesion. It is not racial homogeneity but rather shared values of trust, egalitarianism, and collective responsibility that are a cornerstone of their success. Their commitment to a robust welfare state and equal opportunities predates their recent diversification.

In truth, there are numerous diverse nations with robust welfare systems and high standards of living that challenge the homogeneity theory.

For example, Canada, with its vast ethnic diversity, has a strong health-care system and social safety nets. Likewise, countries in the Caribbean, such as Barbados, have mixed ethnic populations and strong education and health systems.

Our next example is the South American country of Uruguay from roughly 2005 to 2020, including under President José Mujica from 2010 to 2015. Uruguay's tenure under the "Broad Front" coalition stands out as a prominent success, especially against the backdrop of the turmoil experienced by some of its neighbors. This serves as our first reminder that success and failure often are relative to the surrounding circumstances, from a recent baseline, or in contrast to alternative options.[12]

During the period in question, Uruguay underwent significant social reforms. These changes echoed the voice of a progressive society eager for modernization. In 2013, Uruguay legalized same-sex marriage, marking a significant step in the fight for LGBTQ+ rights in the region. In a predominantly Catholic area, the decision to decriminalize abortion in 2012 was indicative of the country's commitment to women's rights. Uruguay also became the first country in the world to fully legalize the production, sale, and consumption of cannabis in 2013, aiming to combat drug-related crimes and treat drug use as a public health, rather than criminal, issue.

While the economic performance of Uruguay during this period might not be labeled as spectacular, it was certainly stable. At a time when neighboring countries such as my birth country of Argentina, or Brazil, faced significant economic challenges, Uruguay showcased resilience. Its GDP grew steadily at an annual rate of about 4.5 percent. Even during global economic downturns, Uruguay showed resilience. For instance, in 2009, when many countries contracted due to the global financial crisis, Uruguay's economy still grew by 2.4 percent. Although Uruguay faced inflationary pressures, it managed to keep inflation relatively in check, maintaining it within the 5 to 9 percent range for most years between 2005 and 2020. Foreign direct investments flowed in, increasing from $250 million in 2005 to a peak of $2.8 billion in 2012, showcasing international confidence in its economic stability and underscoring the global confidence in its economic policies.[13]

The political stability of Uruguay also stood in sharp contrast to the upheavals seen in several neighboring countries. While Venezuela plunged into political crises and Brazil grappled with scandals and institutional challenges, Uruguay's political landscape remained largely scandal-free, transparent, and stable.

Uruguay also made strides in improving its education system, aiming for a more inclusive and equitable structure. Launched in 2007, the Plan Ceibal aimed to bridge the digital divide by providing every primary school student and teacher in Uruguay with a free laptop and Internet connection. By 2009, over four hundred thousand laptops had been distributed, making Uruguay the first country in the world to achieve such a feat. A commitment to education is evident in the country's literacy rates, which by 2010 reached 98 percent among those fifteen years of age and older, one of the highest in the region.[14]

Health and welfare programs were ramped up, reflecting the government's commitment to its citizens' well-being. In 2007, Uruguay implemented its National Integrated Health System, aiming to provide universal health-care coverage. By 2015, over 70 percent of the population was covered under this system.[15] Welfare programs such as "Uruguay Works" and "Family Allowances" were expanded during this period, offering financial assistance to families in need and creating job opportunities for the long-term unemployed.[16] These collective welfare efforts, coupled with economic growth, contributed to a significant reduction in poverty. Between 2005 and 2015, the poverty rate dropped from around 32.5 percent to under 10 percent.[17]

Uruguay's progressive policies and stability did not go unnoticed. International organizations and indices often cited Uruguay as a model for sustainable development, social reforms, and political stability. The era of the Broad Front coalition in Uruguay paints a vivid picture of a nation that successfully melded progressive reforms with economic stability, and is another testament to the potential of left-wing governance to create a balanced, forward-looking, and harmonious society. These were not merely ideological talking points, but actually generated tangible improvements and statistical successes.

Portugal is another country whose left-wing approach has been successful. In 2015, Portugal's political landscape saw a significant shift as the center-right Social Democratic Party, which had been imposing austerity measures in the aftermath of the financial crisis, lost power. A coalition of left-wing parties, including the Socialist Party, Communist Party, Left Bloc, and Greens, took the reins, signaling a departure from the austerity-first policies. They promised to both respect EU fiscal rules and reverse the austerity policies.

As a result, many critics predicted an economic disaster because of the anti-austerity shift, but these fears did not come to fruition. Between 2016 and 2019, Portugal's GDP grew at an average rate of nearly 2.3 percent, outperforming many of its European counterparts and the EU average.[18] Despite rolling back many austerity measures, Portugal saw its budget deficit shrink to less than 1 percent of GDP by 2019, the lowest in over forty years. This was a remarkable achievement, considering that in 2014 the deficit was over 4.4 percent. Portugal also managed to reduce its public debt from 130 percent of GDP in 2014 to around 117 percent in 2019.[19]

Expansion of social and welfare policies also took place, with policies primarily focused on improving the living standards of the Portuguese people. As part of the push to reverse austerity, the government restored public sector wages and pensions that had been cut, increased the minimum wage, and reduced taxes on low earners.[20] Spending on the national health service was increased, aiming to improve the quality and accessibility of health care. The coalition also expanded child benefits and increased the public investment in free textbooks and school meal programs.[21]

In response to rising housing costs and homelessness, especially in cities like Lisbon and Porto, the government launched the Primeiro Direito (First Right) program in 2018. This program aimed to ensure that every citizen had access to adequate housing. By the end of 2019, the program had aided thousands of families, reducing the homeless population and ensuring that many low-income families had access to affordable housing.

Portugal also made impressive strides in renewable energy. In 2016, the country ran for four consecutive days solely on renewable energy, a milestone achievement.[22] By 2019, nearly 54 percent of its electricity came from renewable sources, making it one of the top countries in Europe in this aspect.[23]

Recognizing the importance of sustainable and efficient public transportation, the government increased investments in railways and urban transit systems. By 2019, there was a significant increase in public transit ridership, helping reduce traffic congestion and decrease carbon emissions.[24]

Portugal's successful policies stand in stark contrast to some of its neighbors. While Spain grappled with political instability, with numerous elections and Catalonia's push for independence, Portugal remained politically stable, allowing for consistent policy implementation. Italy, another southern European country, faced political volatility and economic stagnation during the same time period, while Portugal's decisive shift leftward brought about tangible improvements.

Portugal's experience post-2015 serves as yet another confirmation of the viability of left-wing policy in fostering economic growth, improving living standards, and ensuring stability. Their approach offers a template for balancing fiscal responsibility with social welfare. The coalition's tenure demonstrates that it's not about leaning left or right, but about policy efficiency and addressing the needs of the people.

Now moving to another part of the world, we will look at New Zealand, which under Prime Minister Jacinda Ardern saw progressive reforms and the successful handling of COVID, all while maintaining a high standard of living. In fact, Ardern's New Zealand saw some of the most notable and definitive leftward pushes in recent times.

At a budgetary and fiscal level, New Zealand introduced a "Wellbeing Budget" in 2019 focusing on broader indicators than just economic growth. The budget prioritized mental health, child well-being, and domestic violence prevention, allocating significant resources to these areas. Ardern also put forth targets to halve child poverty in the country over a ten-year period. Measures include increasing public housing and implementing free lunches in schools.[25]

New Zealand made major headway with regard to climate initiatives, including with the passage of the Zero Carbon Bill in 2019, with the goal of making New Zealand carbon neutral by 2050. Investments were made in renewable energy, conservation, and sustainable agriculture. New Zealand aims to produce 100 percent renewable electricity by 2035.[26]

Significant investments were made in mental health services, recognizing it as a growing concern. New frontline services were initiated for those with mild to moderate mental health and addiction needs.

With regard to gun safety, Ardern's government quickly passed gun law reforms, banning most semi-automatic weapons and initiating a buyback program after the Christchurch mosque shootings of 2019.[27]

In terms of foreign affairs and trade, Ardern took a proactive role in international diplomacy, advocating for peace, women's rights, and climate change on the global stage. New Zealand also signed the Comprehensive and Progressive Agreement for Trans-Pacific Partnership (CPTPP) to diversify trade and ensure the nation's economic interests.

During the COVID-19 pandemic, New Zealand's swift and effective response was internationally lauded. The country implemented a science-driven approach, which led to some of the lowest per capita COVID-19 case rates and death rates worldwide. Ardern's clear communication and compassionate leadership during this time was noted, reinforcing trust in the government.[28]

Many on the Right will critique New Zealand as an example of progressive success on the basis that New Zealand can afford to be left-wing only because it is a small island nation with a homogeneous population. Upon some basic examination, this retort can easily be defeated. Although it is true that smaller countries may have certain administrative advantages, the size of a nation doesn't determine the effectiveness of progressive policies. Many larger nations with diverse populations, such as Canada and Germany, have implemented progressive policies successfully. Also, smaller nations can face unique challenges. Being an island nation, New Zealand has to grapple with issues of geographic isolation, which can impact trade, tourism, and international collaboration.

New Zealand is also not nearly as homogeneous as may be believed. The country has a significant indigenous Māori population, which makes up about 16.5 percent of the total population. There's also a sizable population of Pacific Islanders, Asians, and other ethnic groups. Historically, New Zealand has grappled with issues of racial and ethnic tensions, particularly related to the rights of the Māori community. Successfully navigating and implementing policies in such a diverse environment refutes the homogeneity argument.

Attributing New Zealand's success under progressive leadership solely to its size or perceived homogeneity oversimplifies the complexities of governance. It's essential to recognize the country's achievements as a

combination of effective leadership, sound policies, and a responsive bu-
reaucracy, rather than just inherent advantages.

Under Jacinda Ardern's leadership, New Zealand experienced a blend
of compassionate governance and pragmatic policymaking. The emphasis on well-being, sustainability, and inclusivity highlights the successful
implementation of left-leaning policies in a modern context. The nation's
accomplishments during her tenure are testament to the viability and effectiveness of such an approach.

Our next country to consider is Germany, specifically in the late twentieth and early twenty-first centuries under the Social Democratic Party
(SPD). Germany under the leadership of Chancellor Gerhard Schröder
and the SPD stands out as a compelling example of successful left-wing
governance in a major European nation. Schröder has been rightly criticized for his connections to Russian energy companies, becoming chair
of the shareholders' committee of Nord Stream AG after leaving office.
Nord Stream AG is the company responsible for the Nord Stream natural
gas pipeline from Russia to Germany. In 2017, Schröder then joined the
board of directors of Rosneft, Russia's largest oil company, and he has also
been involved with Gazprom. There is also much political criticism to be
made of Schröder's connections to these companies and Russian foreign
policy in Crimea. Despite this sometimes common revolving door of politics and industry after leaving office, we will focus on the social democracy
model he followed as chancellor from 1998 to 2005.

Economic reforms such as Agenda 2010 were a cornerstone of
Schröder's government, aiming to revitalize the German economy, which
was struggling with high unemployment and stagnation. The reforms focused on labor market flexibility, welfare state adjustments, and tax reforms. The Agenda 2010 reforms played a significant role in reducing
unemployment rates and increasing Germany's competitiveness on the
global stage. By the time Schröder left office in 2005, Germany's economy
had rebounded, showcasing resilience and stability.[29]

From 2003 to 2007, the country's GDP grew at an average annual
rate of 1.7 percent, a significant improvement from the stagnation of the
previous decade. In comparison to other major European economies, such
as France and the UK, which grew at an average rate of 1.3 percent and

1.1 percent, respectively, during the same period, Germany's performance was notably strong.[30]

One of the most significant achievements of the SPD-led government was the substantial reduction in unemployment. The unemployment rate fell from a peak of 11.2 percent in 2005 to 7.5 percent by the end of 2008. In contrast, other European countries like Spain and Greece saw their unemployment rates soar during the same period, reaching 11.3 percent and 7.7 percent, respectively, by 2008.[31]

Germany solidified its position as a global economic powerhouse, with exports growing from €750 billion in 2003 to over €1 trillion by 2008. The country maintained a substantial trade surplus throughout the first decade of the 2000s, showcasing the competitiveness of its industries on the world stage.[32]

Despite the common criticism that left-wing economic approaches dramatically increase national debts, Germany's public debt as a percentage of GDP was successfully stabilized during the SPD's tenure, hovering around 60 percent by 2005. This was a significant achievement given the rising debt levels in many other European countries during the same period. The Stability and Growth Pact of the European Union mandates that member countries maintain their public debt below 60 percent of GDP, a threshold that Germany managed to adhere to, showcasing fiscal responsibility.

In terms of renewable energy and environmental policy, the Renewable Energy Sources Act (EEG) of 2000 was aimed at boosting renewable energy production, including wind and solar power. It established feed-in tariffs that guaranteed a market for renewable energy, helping Germany become a global leader in clean energy. The SPD-led government emphasized the importance of balancing economic growth with environmental sustainability, laying the groundwork for Germany's growing reputation at the time as a green energy leader, despite backing off such initiatives under subsequent leadership.[33]

On social issues, policies to promote gender equality in the workplace and in society were a focal point, leading to improvements in women's representation and rights. Germany, under the SPD, also worked to better integrate its immigrant population, recognizing the importance of social cohesion and diversity.[34]

While the SPD's time in power was marked by numerous successes, it was not without its challenges and controversies. The Agenda 2010 reforms, in particular, were divisive, with critics arguing that they eroded the welfare state and workers' rights. Nonetheless, the long-term impact of these reforms is often cited as crucial to Germany's subsequent economic stability and growth.

The German example under the SPD highlights the potential for left-wing policies to drive economic revitalization, social progress, and environmental sustainability. It demonstrates that pragmatic, progressive governance can lead to tangible improvements in a nation's economic and social fabric, providing a compelling counterpoint to claims that left-wing politics cannot yield successful outcomes.

We now consider the Kerala state in India, which is a remarkable example of how even within countries, regions that adopt a more progressive or left-wing approach to governance do better, all else being equal. Kerala, located on the southwestern coast of India, is known for its unique social fabric, lush landscapes, and a rich cultural heritage. Despite being one of the smaller states in India, it has consistently stood out for its remarkable social development indices, much of which can be attributed to its long-standing history of left-wing governance. The Kerala state in India has been governed by left-wing parties for many years and has higher literacy, a more advanced public health-care system, greater gender equality, better land reforms and welfare programs, and a more peaceful coexistence of diverse religious traditions, making it a great example of successful regional social democracy within a large country.

The political landscape of Kerala has been predominantly influenced by left-wing ideologies, primarily driven by the Communist Party of India and its allies. To be clear, this is a much further-left ideology than that of this author, but because our approach is empirical rather than simply ideological, the successes in Kerala are worthy of exploration. Since the 1950s, the parties in charge have played a pivotal role in shaping the state's policies, focusing on social justice, equality, and welfare. The Left's commitment to grassroots organization and mobilization has helped consolidate its position in Kerala's political sphere.

Kerala's achievements are nothing short of stunning. Kerala boasts a literacy rate of approximately 94 percent, one of the highest in India.

Kerala's exceptional literacy rate is not a coincidence; it is the result of deliberate and consistent efforts in the field of education. The state government has implemented various progressive education policies aimed at making education accessible and inclusive.[35]

The introduction of child-centric learning methods (in contrast to most of India's teacher-centric approach to education, which relies on lecture and rote memorization, standardized testing, and authoritarian classroom environments) and a focus on critical thinking and creativity have been pivotal. The state revised its school curriculum to make it more contemporary, relevant, and engaging for students. Significant investment has been made in training teachers and enhancing their skills. This ensures that educators are well equipped to handle diverse classrooms and cater to the needs of all students. Kerala has consistently worked toward improving the infrastructure of its educational institutions. This includes well-maintained classrooms, libraries stocked with a variety of learning resources, and the provision of modern teaching aids.

Access is also a major factor. The Kerala government has worked to remove barriers to education, including initiatives to provide free textbooks, uniforms, and midday meals to students, and ensuring that financial constraints do not hinder a child's ability to learn.

Kerala's health-care system is often hailed as one of the best in the country. With an extensive network of public hospitals and clinics, the state ensures accessible and affordable health care for its residents. This focus on public health has led to impressive outcomes, including high life expectancy and low infant mortality rates.[36]

The state has a dense network of public health-care facilities, ensuring that even the most remote areas have access to medical care. There has been a strong focus on preventive health care, with numerous programs aimed at educating the public on healthy living practices, sanitation, and disease prevention. The government has worked to make health care accessible and affordable for all. This includes the provision of free or subsidized medical treatment, medicines, and diagnostic services. Significant resources have been invested in upgrading the health-care infrastructure, ensuring that medical facilities are well equipped and staffed.

Looking at land policy, in the early years of its governance, the left-wing administration implemented radical land reforms, redistributing land to the landless and ensuring secure tenancy for farmers. These reforms addressed historical inequalities and laid the groundwork for social harmony and economic stability.[37]

Kerala's economy is unique, with a significant reliance on remittances from its large diaspora and a strong presence of the service sector. While the state has seen steady economic growth, critics argue that it has not matched the pace of other Indian states. However, it is essential to note that Kerala's focus has been on sustainable and inclusive growth, ensuring that development benefits all sections of society.

Without question, despite its successes, Kerala faces challenges, particularly in terms of job creation and industrial growth. The high unemployment rate is a concern, and there is a need for innovative policies to drive economic diversification and generate employment opportunities. The state's administration is aware of these issues and is working toward addressing them, keeping in line with its commitment to social welfare. As we've already considered earlier, success and failure must be evaluated contextually, and in this situation, the context is a broader economic situation in India that has been less than ideal for decades.

The "Kerala model" of development, characterized by high social development and moderate economic growth, stands as a testament to the potential of left-wing governance. It demonstrates that prioritizing social welfare does not hinder progress but rather lays a strong foundation for a just and equitable society.

Kerala's advancement under left-wing governance provides valuable insights into the transformative power of policies centered around social justice and welfare. It shows that with the right priorities, governments can drive social change, improve living standards, and foster an environment of inclusivity and equality. Compare the 73 percent literacy rate of Uttar Pradesh; the infant mortality rate in Bihar, which is three times that of Kerala; or the limited gender equality, lower female literacy rate, and higher gender violence rate in Rajasthan, among other possible statistics.[38] The success of Kerala's model reinforces the argument that left-wing policies, far from being impractical or detrimental, can lead to holistic and sustainable development.

Now having seen a number of progressive success stories, we will consider the most important overarching meta-issues that impact and potentially drown out whatever specific issues readers might be most interested in.

For example, if one cares about abortion, or education, or access to health care, accomplishing change in those areas depends at some basic level on how politics is financed and how elected officials are chosen. Climate change is a factor because if climate change isn't dealt with, there won't be a functional planet on which to be an activist for those issues. And if people don't have access to health care, they may be unable to obtain treatment in order to be healthy activists in the real world, or their activism can be derailed by family members, friends, or loved ones being sick without access to health care. These concerns layer on top of all other political issues.

MONEY IN POLITICS

Jasper McChesney from the nonpartisan nonprofit United Republican found that in congressional races, the candidate who raises more money wins 91 percent of the time.[39] Raising more money allows the purchase of more media time and advertisements across multiple platforms.

The unfortunate reality is that the concept of "money talks" applies to politics, and its voice often overshadows that of the electorate. The role of campaign finance in modern American politics is undeniable, wielding influence over policymaking, legislative decisions, and even the narratives surrounding elections. The ways in which campaigns are funded can often serve as a bellwether for the priorities and potential allegiances of candidates and political parties.

The origins and evolution of campaign finance in the United States amount to a convoluted tale. While America's Founding Fathers held concerns about the influence of money in politics, it wasn't until the Progressive Era of the early twentieth century that the first campaign finance laws were enacted. Later landmark legislation such as the Federal Election Campaign Act (FECA) of 1971 set the groundwork for modern campaign finance regulation. However, subsequent Supreme Court decisions, most notably *Citizens United v. FEC* in 2010, dramatically altered the campaign finance landscape, allowing unlimited corporate and union spending in elections and giving rise to super PACs (political action committees). This correlation raises unsettling questions about the essence of democracy when financial clout becomes a dominant factor in electoral success.

Campaign finance considerations continue to exert influence well beyond Election Day. PACs and super PACs stand as towering figures in the campaign finance realm. While individual donation limits to campaigns exist, these entities offer a detour. Super PACs especially can raise unlimited funds from corporations, unions, and individuals and then spend unlimited sums to overtly advocate for or against political candidates. This mechanism effectively circumvents the traditional donation caps. The twist in the tale is the emergence of "dark money"—funds donated to nonprofit organizations that can spend unlimited amounts on political campaigns without disclosing their donors, rendering the origins of these massive funds mysterious.

While leftist movements like End Citizens United aim to reverse this decision, there's a burgeoning sentiment that the solution might not lie in overturning *Citizens United* at all. Instead, alternative reforms like introducing public financing of campaigns, enhancing transparency in donor disclosures, and setting up a system of small donor matching funds have been proposed as potential remedies.

The story of campaign finance in the US serves as a cautionary tale of the challenges democracies face in the modern age. As long as the influence of money remains unchecked, questions about the very nature of American democracy—whether it serves the many or the few—will persist. Addressing the distortions introduced by unchecked campaign finance is fundamental to restoring faith in the democratic process and ensuring that the voice of the electorate is not drowned out by the deafening roar of money.

HOW ELECTIONS ARE RUN

Our electoral systems don't just pick our leaders; they also shape the very fabric of our policy decisions for years to come. Whether it's the priorities of education reform, the nuances of reproductive rights, or the legislative approach to environmental concerns, the policies are affected by the champions we select through these systems to carry our hopes, concerns, and demands to the legislative arenas. But if the system that selects these champions is flawed or skewed, it casts a shadow over every decision they make. It means the issues that resonate with the majority could be sidelined due to the interests of a few. It's a reminder that for genuine change in specific issues close to our hearts, understanding and potentially reforming our electoral systems is paramount.

One of the systems currently in place, first past the post (FPTP), rewards the candidate with the most votes in a given area, even if they don't secure a majority. While simple and direct, FPTP can sometimes be criticized for not truly representing the will of all voters, particularly in multicandidate races. It can lead to the "spoiler effect," where third-party candidates siphon off votes, potentially altering the outcome.

FPTP has an inherent tendency to solidify the dominance of major parties, pushing political dynamics toward a two-party system. This can stifle innovative ideas and progressive agendas proposed by emerging third parties, making systemic change slower and more difficult. With the winner-takes-all nature of FPTP, there's often a rush to fund the most "electable" candidates, which usually translates to those with the most financial backing from the start. Candidates with less initial financial support, even if they have innovative ideas, face an uphill battle to gain visibility. This dynamic naturally privileges wealthy donors and interests, as their chosen candidates are more likely to win in the FPTP system.

Knowing that third-party or fringe candidates have little to no chance of winning in an FPTP system, voters might either abstain from voting (believing their vote won't matter) or vote strategically for a "lesser evil" rather than their genuine first choice. This can lead to an electorate that's disengaged and disillusioned.

Also, in FPTP, the majority wins, but that majority might only be a plurality (e.g., 40 percent of the vote), except in jurisdictions that have established runoff rules requiring a candidate to reach 50 percent to avoid triggering a runoff election between the top vote-getters. This means that, barring a runoff rule, a significant percentage of the electorate might feel unrepresented. In areas where one party always wins, there's little incentive for opposition parties to engage with the community or for the dominant party to listen to minority voices.

One alternative is proportional representation (PR), which aims to allocate seats in proportion to the votes received. This means that smaller parties or interest groups can gain representation based on their proportion of the vote. PR arguably offers a more holistic reflection of a populace's desires and can lead to more collaborative politics as coalition governments often form. Despite these benefits, PR can sometimes cause new problems to be dealt with, particularly when extremist far-right parties end up achieving some level of representation or being included in coalitions, when in an FPTP system they would end up with zero representation.

A potentially better alternative is ranked-choice voting (RCV), also known as instant-runoff voting. RCV allows voters to rank candidates in order of preference. If no candidate receives a majority of the vote on the first count, the candidate with the least votes is eliminated, and their votes are redistributed based on second choices. This process continues until a candidate secures a majority. RCV can help eliminate the spoiler effect and ensures that the winning candidate has a broader base of support. It can also encourage candidates to appeal to a wider range of voters, potentially leading to more moderate and collaborative politics.

RCV can help reflect a more genuine will of the people, ensuring that votes are not wasted and that minority voices have a chance to be heard. It also encourages more candidates to participate without the fear of being a "spoiler" and can lead to more civil campaign discourse as candidates are less likely to alienate supporters of their rivals.

FPTP, while straightforward, can sometimes perpetuate a political environment where money and major parties dominate, innovative ideas are stifled, and a large portion of the electorate feels unrepresented or forced to vote strategically rather than genuinely.

Another systemic issue is the Electoral College. The Electoral College system used in US presidential elections is one of the worst aspects of American democracy, and is in fact fundamentally antidemocratic. Its defenders argue it balances power among states, ensuring smaller states aren't overshadowed by more populous ones. However, it's an antiquated system that sometimes leads to outcomes where a candidate—usually a Democratic candidate—wins the popular vote but loses the presidency.

The Electoral College was established by the framers of the US Constitution as a compromise between election of the president by Congress and election by popular vote. One justification was fear of the "tyranny of the majority" wherein the framers were wary of direct democracy, fearing that a charismatic tyrant could manipulate public opinion and come to power.

There was also the concern about representation for smaller states. The framers wanted to ensure that less populous states had a voice in the

presidential election, thus preventing larger states from having disproportionate influence. They also thought that the Electoral College would
encourage candidates to visit the smaller states, rather than focus only on
densely populated urban areas. In the pre-media era, it was far more difficult to learn about candidates without their physical presence.

The reasoning that originally justified the Electoral College is now
substantially obsolete. In the age of rapid communication and national
media, state-specific issues are less pronounced in presidential campaigns
than national ones. Modern democratic institutions, checks and balances,
and an informed electorate make the original fears of a tyrannical majority less pertinent. Most states award all their electors to the candidate who
wins the popular vote in that state, regardless of the margin. This means
that a candidate could theoretically win the presidency with a very small
number of actual voters supporting them.

Further, candidates still focus their attention on a small number of
states, but it is a different group of states than it was in the past. Candidates now focus time and resources on a small number of competitive
states, called swing or battleground states, often neglecting the issues of
voters in states that are safely Democratic or Republican. This orients
policy discussions and promises toward a fraction of the electorate, and
the issues that result have led many to call for the elimination of the Electoral College in favor of a direct popular vote or a vote compact (discussed
further in chapter 7).

Before we even reach the Electoral College, however, we have the
issue of primaries, which play a critical role in the American electoral
process, essentially acting as a filter to determine who makes it to the
main electoral stage. These can often be dominated by party stalwarts
or by those with significant financial backing, potentially sidelining fresh
voices or grassroots-supported candidates. Primary elections often see
significantly lower voter turnout than general elections. This means that
a relatively small, and sometimes more ideologically extreme, portion of
the electorate can determine a party's nominee. In the summer of 2024,
another scenario presented itself in which, after securing the Democratic
nomination, President Joe Biden decided not to pursue reelection, and
Vice President Kamala Harris became the presumptive nominee prior
to the Democratic National Convention after pursuing and securing the
support of Democratic delegates.

Primaries, especially closed primaries where only registered party members can vote, can push candidates to appeal to their party's most fervent base. This can lead to the nomination of more polarizing and ideologically extreme candidates and also further division in the general election. On the other hand, open primaries, where voters from any party can participate, are vulnerable to "raiding." This is when members of one party vote in the other party's primary to try to select a weaker or more polarizing candidate, making the general election easier for the candidate that they genuinely prefer.

Addressing primary issues through various reforms could lead to more representative, less polarizing, less extreme candidates, which in turn might reflect a broader spectrum of voter interests and values in the general election.

Another way the Right has attempted to win elections without actually winning the hearts and minds of voters is through voter suppression tactics. Voter suppression refers to tactics employed to deter or prevent specific groups of people from voting, undermining the principle of fair and equal representation in a democracy. Such tactics include stringent voter ID laws, which disproportionately affect certain populations, purging voter rolls, limiting early and absentee voting, closing or relocating polling places, and using disinformation and intimidation.

Voter ID laws require voters to present specific forms of identification that are less commonly held by certain groups, particularly minorities and the economically disadvantaged. In many cases, these laws disproportionately affect Black and Latino voters, as well as young voters and seniors. Although the IDs themselves may be free, they can often require non-free documents or copies of documents in order to obtain the voter IDs, or they necessitate travel to specific areas during business hours, often requiring standing in line for a long time, which overwhelmingly impacts rural voters, poor voters, and workers who cannot afford to take time off during business hours to get a voter ID.[40]

Purging voter rolls is the removal of voters from registration lists under the pretense of keeping them updated. In some instances, eligible voters are incorrectly removed, a phenomenon that became a point of contention in states like Georgia during the 2018 midterm elections. Sometimes voter rolls are only reviewed and purged in specific areas, as calculated to provide a particular advantage to one party or candidate.[41]

Reducing the number of days for early voting or setting stringent conditions for absentee voting can suppress turnout, particularly among those who can't get to the polls on Election Day. Closing or relocating polling places can result in longer lines and inconvenience for voters. Often these closures occur in minority or economically disadvantaged neighborhoods.

Spreading false information about voting requirements or procedures can deter voters, such as announcing that there is a voter ID requirement when there actually is not, or spreading false information about voting days, times, or locations. There's also the use of intimidation tactics at polling places, like aggressive poll watching, which can scare off voters. These tactics are often, strictly speaking, illegal, but a lack of enforcement, or delayed enforcement, often leads to their use.

The 2020 election saw an unprecedented focus on voter suppression, with the Trump campaign and its allies employing several tactics. The Trump campaign repeatedly claimed, without evidence, that mail-in voting would lead to massive fraud.[42] This created distrust in a voting method essential during a pandemic. The US Postal Service, critical for mail-in voting, faced defunding and operational changes that led to delays, raising concerns about whether ballots would be received and counted in time. The Trump campaign filed numerous lawsuits in multiple states attempting to block or invalidate certain types of votes or to stop vote counting altogether.

A number of progressive reforms such as providing clear, authoritative information on voting procedures, requirements, and rights can help counteract false narratives and reinstate our right to vote. Oversight and legislation, like the Voting Rights Act, once a powerful tool against voter suppression, was gutted by the Supreme Court in 2013. Restoring its full powers, or passing new federal legislation, could provide essential protections against suppression efforts.

Gerrymandering is another way to suppress the vote through the art, or science, or scam, of drawing electoral boundaries to favor one party over another. This is arguably one of the most significant challenges facing genuine democratic representation. By creating "safe" districts for one party, gerrymandering can diminish the competitive nature of elections, leaving citizens with little true choice and sometimes feeling their votes don't matter. By creatively drawing district lines, the party in power can maximize its electoral prospects and minimize those of its opposition.

Both Democrats and Republicans have used gerrymandering, but historically, gerrymandering has benefited Republicans more due to a combination of population distribution factors and opportunities to do the gerrymandering itself.

There are two primary techniques used in gerrymandering, known as "packing" and "cracking."

Packing involves concentrating as many voters of one type as possible into a single electoral district to reduce their influence in other districts. For instance, if party A knows that a particular area has a heavy concentration of party B supporters, they might pack all of those voters into one district, ensuring party B wins that particular district by a large margin but diluting its influence elsewhere.

Cracking is the opposite of packing. It involves spreading out voters of a particular type among many districts to dilute their influence and prevent them from achieving a majority in any one district. By "cracking" the opposition's voter base into pieces and spreading them thinly across multiple districts, party A can ensure that party B doesn't have enough voters in any given district to secure a win.

For example, in North Carolina in 2016, the state's congressional map was deemed to be racially gerrymandered by Republicans, with boundaries drawn to diminish the electoral influence of Black voters. This led to legal challenges and a mandate to redraw the districts.

Gerrymandering is a powerful tool that can fundamentally skew the representation of a population. It allows politicians to "choose their voters" rather than the other way around. A number of reforms and alternatives to the current system exist, and addressing this problem is crucial for a fair and representative democracy, especially as sophisticated technology and data analysis make it possible to gerrymander with even more precision.

CLIMATE CHANGE

At its core, the climate crisis affects every facet of human society. If it is left unchecked, many currently populated areas of the world will become uninhabitable. Coastal cities could be submerged, interior regions could be stricken by drought, and societal structures could be disrupted by frequent natural disasters. Under such conditions, activism for other causes becomes secondary, if not impossible. It's not merely about the environment but the very stage on which all human endeavors, including activism, play out. If the stage collapses, all acts, irrespective of their nature, come to a premature end.

The Industrial Revolution marked the beginning of a massive increase in greenhouse gas emissions due to the burning of fossil fuels. Over the subsequent two centuries, as industries expanded and deforestation continued, the concentration of greenhouse gases in our atmosphere surged, leading to a rapid rise in global temperatures. Human activities have accelerated the pace of climate change, pushing our planet into uncharted and dangerous territory.

The impact of climate change on society is varied and widespread. Environmental elements include melting ice caps, rising sea levels, extreme weather events, and significant temperature increases in some areas. Economic impacts include effects on agriculture, where climate change can lead to crop failures and food shortages. Trade can be disrupted and global economies depressed. Climate change also impacts migration. As regions become uninhabitable due to droughts, floods, or other climate-related catastrophes, we witness a surge in climate refugees. There is also an important health component, as increasing temperatures can lead to the spread of tropical diseases, and extreme weather events can strain health-care systems.

The conversation around climate change is inherently fraught from the start as a result of much of the American right wing refusing to even acknowledge that climate change is happening. Even when they acknowledge it is happening, they will often deny that human activities on earth, such as industrialization, have any impact on climate change. Much of this denial stems from the belief from many on the Right that if they were to acknowledge that climate change is happening and is influenced by human activities, the policy prescription would be immutably fixed. In reality, acknowledgment of climate change caused by humans would simply be the start of the conversation about how it should be addressed.

Policy considerations include mitigation versus adaptation. While mitigation focuses on reducing the causes of climate change (like reducing emissions), adaptation emphasizes adjusting to its effects. International cooperation would likely be a major piece of properly dealing with climate change. The global nature of the issue means that solutions require cooperation. Accords like the Paris Agreement aim for collective action, but the political will is paramount. A transition to green renewable energy would undoubtedly play a major role, shifting away from fossil fuels, but this transition needs to consider workers in traditional energy sectors.

A number of reform ideas exist and have been studied extensively, but the political will to act in a significant way on these ideas is still lacking. Comprehensive legislation from the Left like the Green New Deal proposal that addresses both climate change and economic inequality is one approach. Carbon taxes, where a price is put on carbon emissions, can provide an economic incentive to reduce greenhouse gas emissions. Investment in research to make green energy more efficient and affordable should be heavily funded and supported. Large-scale projects to plant trees and restore lost forests, including afforestation and reforestation, can have a major impact on the planet's ability to absorb carbon dioxide. Promoting farming practices that are both environmentally friendly and economically viable as a way to make agriculture more sustainable can be approached in a number of ways. Lastly, education is a major aspect of this discussion. Raising awareness about the issue and its implications, creating a more informed and engaged citizenry, will also encourage the public to demand that our elected officials do something about the problem.

Climate change is not just an environmental issue, but also an economic, social, and health issue. Its cascading effects on various facets of our society make it one of the major challenges of our time. Addressing it isn't just about saving the planet but ensuring that the stage for all human activity, including activism, remains intact.

HEALTH CARE

Beyond its direct implications for well-being, health care serves as the bedrock of societal participation, including activism. Without a healthy populace, the very fabric of proactive societal change is threatened.

A basic level of health is the first requirement for any form of societal participation. When individuals grapple with health issues, or when they're ensnared in medical debts, their ability to partake in activism dwindles.

The journey of health-care access in the United States traces from rudimentary physician visits in the colonial era to the complex web of insurance, public programs, and medical institutions today. Despite attempts at many points in American history, including during the early twentieth century, to dramatically increase access to health care, the American system still leaves many behind, or provides them services but then saddles them with crushing medical debt, sometimes leading to bankruptcy. Landmark legislation, such as the Affordable Care Act, aimed to bridge the divide, yet disparities remain.

There are also important economic ramifications to inadequate health-care access. Financial strains from health care often render individuals incapable of active participation in the economy itself as both workers and consumers. Many face the dilemma of choosing between a medical procedure and daily expenses. The weight of medical expenses can leave little room for participation in larger societal issues.

There is also an intersection of mental health and activism. Activism is as much a mental endeavor as it is physical. Activists often grapple with stress, trauma, and even burnout. Lack of access to mental health care can incapacitate the most fervent advocates. For instance, civil rights activists, exposed to constant confrontation and sometimes violence, deeply benefit from psychological support, underscoring the importance of mental health care in the activism sphere.

The goal of equitable health care remains elusive in the United States, although improvements have been made. Disparities based on race, income, and geography persist, creating hierarchies within activism. Marginalized communities, already grappling with health-care access, find it doubly hard to champion causes, further perpetuating cycles of inequality. When those with access to health care are more likely to be healthy enough to be and remain activists, the desires of the group that has access to health care becomes more likely to be made policy and be listened to by our elected officials.

Many reform ideas have been proposed when it comes to health care. It is beyond the scope of this chapter and book to dive as deeply as one could into this issue, and many important books have been written about health-care reform. However, some ideas are worthy of individual mention.

Universal health care or single-payer systems are one option, adopting a system where health care is a right, not a privilege. Another approach is the expansion of Medicaid and Medicare, broadening the umbrella of these programs to cover more individuals. Canada has a publicly funded and primarily publicly administered system, where health services are provided by private entities, ensuring universal coverage for all Canadian citizens. France employs a combination of public and private providers, with compulsory health insurance that reimburses patients for a significant portion of their health-care costs; the French system is often regarded as one of the best health-care systems globally. Germany has a multipayer system based on mandatory health insurance, where both private and public insurance programs coexist, providing comprehensive coverage to nearly all residents.

Singapore's unique system blends government regulation and subsidies, mandatory individual savings, and a variety of public and private insurance programs, resulting in high-quality care with controlled costs. In the United Kingdom, the system is publicly funded through tax revenues and delivered by the National Health Service (NHS), offering comprehensive medical services to all residents, free at the point of use.

None of these systems is perfect, but all can serve as at least partial models for making improvements to the American system, which works perfectly well for the wealthy and upper middle class, but quite poorly for many others.

Policies to reduce drug prices tackle another element of what can make comprehensive health care unaffordable by making medications accessible and affordable to all. The Biden administration made progress on this by bringing pharmaceutical manufacturers of the most widely prescribed drugs to the table to negotiate discounts for Medicare recipients.

Other proposals include mental health parity, which would ensure that mental health treatment is given the same importance and priority as physical health in insurance plans. Lastly, community health clinics can be put in place to bolster these grassroots health-care hubs to reach the most marginalized.

For a society to thrive and for its members to champion causes close to their hearts, the sine qua non is a robust health-care system. The correlation between health care and activism is inextricable. Only when we ensure that every individual, irrespective of their background, has access to quality health care can we hope for a society that's actively engaged in shaping its future.

Leftism, contrary to the misinformed rhetoric of its critics on the right, does not stifle innovation or economic prosperity. Instead, it fosters an environment where both can thrive. The high standards of living, comprehensive social safety nets, and robust economies of social democracies debunk the myth that social welfare and economic strength are mutually exclusive. These nations consistently rank highly in global indices for happiness, standard of living, and ease of doing business, providing a tangible metric of success.

Social democracy, built from leftist thinking, provides a middle path, combining the innovative potential of the market with a strong commitment to social welfare. It is living proof that governments can be both pro-business and pro-people. By ensuring that the benefits of economic growth are shared broadly, social democracy contributes to social cohesion and political stability.

As we reflect on the numerous examples of successful left-wing governments in other places and times and contextualize what's at stake in terms of our activism and political goals, it becomes evident that social democracy in the US is not a utopian fantasy but rather a series of practical reforms that address some of the most pressing issues of our time.

In an era marked by rising inequality, environmental degradation, and political polarization, the principles of leftism offer a beacon of hope and a viable path forward. They underscore the possibility of creating societies that are not only prosperous but also just, inclusive, and resilient. This is not just a political choice—it is a pledge to future generations. It is a testament to our ability to learn from history, adapt to changing circumstances, and work together for the common good. As we move forward, let us embrace the lessons from these left-wing successes, and strive to build a world that is equitable, sustainable, and prosperous for all.

CHAPTER 6

HOW TO FIGHT AGAINST A MOVEMENT THAT HAS NO POLICY

Dating back decades, but noticeably more so since Newt Gingrich's takeover of the House of Representatives in 1994, the Republican Party has shifted to ignoring policy and being instead about cultural battles, public relations, and character assassination of their political opponents. This reached new highs during the Trump era, with entire candidacies and tenures in elected office based solely around making the Left look bad, spreading salacious but corrosive disinformation, and building a house of cards on the flimsiest foundations of rumor and innuendo. Ignored completely have been real policy issues and questions, including how to get people health care and housing, how to repair our education system, what to do about climate change and pollution, what a twenty-first-century foreign policy should look like, and what we want our country's role in the world to be.

The Republican shift away from policy and toward cultural issues, memes, and pablum can be traced all the way back to the Civil Rights Movement. Although not discussed in our historical narrative thus far, after the passage of the 1964 Civil Rights Act, the American right wing began a shift away from substantive policy focus, supplanting it with preying on fears and prejudices in the context of the societal move away from racial segregation and discrimination. Ronald Reagan's campaign and presidency built on this with the racially tinged fear-mongering around welfare programs and the modification of the War on Poverty into a war against the poor.[1]

When Congressman Gingrich became Speaker of the House in 1995, during the presidency of Bill Clinton, the stakes were raised dramatically on the politics of personal attacks. Then, George W. Bush, as a result of both his constituency and the general pseudo- and anti-intellectual direction of the Republican Party, signaled a more noticeable shift in the same direction, fomenting remarkable disdain for education as a badge of honor among many of his supporters. In the Bush era, there were still ostensibly policy-based priorities among some Republicans, including related to taxes (keeping them low, especially for the rich), regulation of businesses (limiting regulation as much as possible), education (despite No Child Left Behind being denounced by public educators as an attack on public education rather than a support of it), foreign policy (usually in favor of military interventions), and against gay marriage and abortion. However, they were approached in an increasingly simplistic manner and over time were pushed aside by cultural issues.

The election of President Barack Obama opened the proverbial floodgates for the American Right to abandon the pretense of caring about policy almost completely. The xenophobic and racist contingent of the American Right saw Obama's election as an open door to the total abandonment of policy. This period saw the rise of the "birther" movement, which argued that Obama was not born in the US and was thus ineligible to be president, as well as equally disturbing but less popular conspiracy theories. As it happened, Donald Trump was a key promoter of the birther movement, seamlessly leading directly into a major point in the policy-less time line: the Trump era.

The culmination of Barack Obama's two terms ultimately welcomed the election of Donald Trump in 2016, at which point any pretense of policy evaporated completely. During Trump's 2016 campaign, there were vague allusions to policy, including "fixing trade," "building the wall," "being tough on China," replacing Obamacare with a "beautiful" plan,[2] and the like, but it was clear to those paying attention that there was no actual way to achieve the things that Donald Trump promised.

By the 2018 midterm elections, and even more noticeably in Donald Trump's ultimately failed 2020 reelection campaign, Republican echo politics was empty and vapid. The 2020 campaign was based on fighting nonexistent "socialism" and "communism," "protecting" suburbs from some never completely clear threat believed to involve non-White people, opposing critical race theory, not allowing supposedly fascist Democrats to put in place public health guidelines to limit the spread of the COVID-19 pandemic, as well as some dabbling in xenophobia and transphobia, and the baseless claims of a broad Democratic plot for Joe Biden to steal the 2020 election from Donald Trump through some combination of mail-in voting and COVID guidelines. Without exaggeration, Donald Trump alleged on the campaign trail that Joe Biden would change energy policy resulting in no indoor heating or cooling, that he would end the suburbs, and that he would plunge the country into a depression.[3] However, despite the failure of this approach for Trump in 2020, it is a strategy that sometimes works for Republicans.

Notably, many 2022 Republican candidates were able to win with completely substance-free campaigns. Examples include Marjorie Taylor Greene, Lauren Boebert, and many others. Greene has been a vocal proponent of a variety of conspiracy theories, and spends most of her time in office and on the campaign trail talking about impeaching President Joe Biden, communism, socialism, and other inflammatory rhetoric. Boebert vaguely touched on the policy issue of firearms, but has mostly emphasized cultural and identity politics over policy matters.

"Socialism" as an attack is a particularly instructive example. The Republican Party has trained its base to see anything to the left of their own party as "socialism." They decry the agenda of center-left President Joe Biden as being "far left," "socialist," and even "communist" without even understanding what these terms mean, and their voters willingly take the bait. When they are asked to define these terms, they can't, but they know it's bad, and they know it applies to Biden.

Beyond the effectiveness of this tactic is the ironic, if not depressing, reality that endless droves of Republican voters enjoy the fruits of so-called socialist safety nets and social programs, often without recognizing it. The classic lines, possibly apocryphal at this point, of Republican Medicare recipients screaming that the "socialist Democrats should get the government's hands off my Medicare" stretch credulity but are an all-too-real representation of the confusion afflicting Republican voters. In the process of conducting interviews at Trump rallies between 2021 and 2023, our own *David Pakman Show* correspondents have interviewed MAGA supporters who were furious about Biden's "socialism." One

Trump supporter, interviewed by Right Side Broadcasting Network, complained about the "socialist" policies of President Biden and Democrats, while simultaneously explaining that "fortunately" he is on Medicare, and also has VA benefits as a veteran—a stunning cognitive dissonance.[4]

Also during the Trump era, the Republican Party became remarkably more adept at weaponizing social media and other platforms with a relentless obsession with contrived viral stories, again at the continued exclusion of serious policy proposals. The administration often used X, the platform formerly known as Twitter, as an official means of communication.[5] Often, these tweets were designed not to announce policy but to ignite culture wars. The potency of the tweet over substantive policy discussions cannot be overstated. By dominating the news cycle with incendiary tweets, Trump effectively diverted attention from real policy debates.

It would be a disservice to ignore the role of populist rhetoric in this discourse degradation. As has come up in other contexts, it's important to remember that populism is primarily a rhetoric, not an ideology or set of policy prescriptions. Traditional conservatism did have associated with it a more fixed set of policy ideas, but as Trump turned the Republican Party's public-facing platform into a more populist-sounding one, the abandonment of policy was a natural outcome. The generic populist rhetoric of being "for the middle class," being "anti-establishment outsiders," and being in a crisis that must be solved by strong leaders was the perfect distraction for the MAGA Trumpist right wing from serious policy discussions.

As is often the case, this rhetoric is combined with a strongman authoritarian—in this case Trump—and mixed together with the rejection of experts, the addition of a victimhood complex, and a focus on nationalism and identity. The end result becomes a growing indifference not only among the politicians, but also among their followers—in this case Republican voters—to substantive policy.

Much of the success of such a pathetic strategy is the result of a structural advantage that the right wing maintains, which we will shortly explore, but it first must be understood that when it comes to the opinions of the American people, the right wing has actually lost on policy. As a result, they've abandoned policy completely, which explains where we are today. Let's consider a few important areas.

HEALTH CARE

As health-care costs have continued to increase, a significant majority of Americans now favor at least the option of a government health-care system, all driven by the belief that governments have the responsibility to provide some basic level of health care to everyone, regardless of ability to pay. A 2020 poll by Pew Research, a reputable nonpartisan think tank, found that 63 percent of Americans support this view.[6] A Kaiser Family Foundation poll found that two-thirds of Americans support a public health insurance option to compete with private health insurance plans.[7]

The concept of a government plan, and at minimum some government involvement in health insurance, is not a fringe idea limited to the supposed far left. Rather, there is actual consensus building in the United States that health care should not be a privilege dictated by one's financial standing.

ABORTION

The overturning of *Roe v. Wade* in 2022 by the most right-wing Supreme Court in decades could have been interpreted as a reflection of broader public sentiment about abortion and its legality and accessibility. In reality, the opposite is true. The country has become continually more supportive of abortion rights over time. A 2019 NPR/PBS NewsHour/ Marist poll found that three-quarters of Americans want to keep *Roe v. Wade*, the landmark Supreme Court ruling that legalized abortion nationwide, in place.[8] A 2020 study by Pew Research indicated that a substantial 61 percent of Americans were of the conviction that abortion should be legal, whether in all scenarios or at least in most cases.[9]

Medical advancements have demystified and destigmatized abortion, and the understanding of abortion as an issue of fundamental autonomy over one's own body has pushed support of legal abortion further into the mainstream.

Although it is a topic for separate discussion, the rolling back of *Roe v. Wade* at a time when support for legal abortion is at its highest level in the *Roe v. Wade* era serves as a reminder of another broken element of American politics: the disconnect between what voters want and what elected officials will actually push for, in this case indirectly through President

Donald Trump's nominations of right-wing justices to the Supreme Court, who ultimately participated in overturning *Roe v. Wade*.[10]

GAY MARRIAGE

Acceptance of gay marriage has consistently risen. The cultural and social progress regarding gay rights and acceptance can be traced through various milestones, of which public sentiment is a significant barometer. A testament to this transformational change in societal values is reflected in polling data. By 2020, a Gallup poll illuminated the reality that a record 67 percent of Americans expressed their support for same-sex marriage.[11] This number is particularly poignant when one contrasts it with data from just two decades prior when a majority of Americans opposed the idea.

Several factors can be credited for this monumental shift. Pioneering advocates and visible figures from the LGBTQ+ community humanized the struggle for gay rights, allowing many to see beyond prejudices. The entertainment industry, literature, and media began portraying LGBTQ+ characters and stories with depth and authenticity, further normalizing and celebrating diverse expressions of love. Legal victories, most notably the Supreme Court's landmark decision in *Obergefell v. Hodges* in 2015, not only ratified same-sex marriage nationwide but also bolstered its societal acceptance.

TAXES AND THE WEALTH GAP

Americans increasingly believe that the tax code favors the wealthy and that raising taxes on the wealthiest is the appropriate approach to reduce wealth inequality. According to a 2017 Pew Research poll, over 60 percent of Americans said that what bothers them about the tax system is the belief that wealthy people and corporations don't pay their fair share.[12] A Hill-HarrisX poll from 2019 found that 74 percent of registered voters supported increasing taxes on the wealthy.[13] A 2020 Reuters/Ipsos poll found that 64 percent of respondents agreed that the very rich should contribute an extra share of their total wealth each year to support public programs.[14]

ENVIRONMENT AND CLIMATE CHANGE

Americans accept the science of climate change and believe that not enough is being done about the issue. A 2020 Pew Research poll found that two-thirds of Americans felt the government was doing too little to reduce the effects of climate change. Seventy-nine percent of Americans believed the country should prioritize developing alternative energy sources over expanding oil, gas, and coal.[15] A 2021 Yale Climate Opinion study found that 57 percent of Americans even believe global warming is mostly caused by human activities, which although lower, is still notable given the amount of effort expended by climate deniers to disabuse the American people of this belief.[16]

GUN SAFETY REGULATIONS

Despite the view from the Republican Party that any new gun safety regulations or restrictions of any kind are tantamount to a violation of the Second Amendment, Americans actually favor many such regulations. Numerous polls, including those from Quinnipiac University, Gallup, and Pew Research, consistently showed strong public support for measures such as universal background checks (around 90 percent support) and bans on assault-style weapons (50–60 percent support).[17]

When looking at any one poll or public opinion survey, it's important to consider the wording, the motivations for the poll, and its funding, but the broader trend is clear: while the Republican Party has remained recalcitrant in the context of public opinion shifting left on every major issue over the last several decades, the voters have fallen increasingly out of step with what the GOP has been offering. This must be understood as another motivation for their platform having abandoned policy. The policies they do favor are political losers in a country whose voters resemble northern European social democrats more and more.

This is not to say that the country has become "extremely left-wing" or that no reactionary conservatism remains. The US is a country of more than 330 million people, and although the electorate has moved left on many issues by several percentage points, this still leaves tens of millions of Americans favoring and believing a variety of right-wing positions. Furthermore, especially compared to northern European countries, the

US remains more individualistic and, in many economic areas, more conservative, than many other countries.

However, this policy loss is another major factor in explaining and understanding why Republicans increasingly run campaigns on social issues and contrived grievances.

The Left is at a notable disadvantage, and the Right at an advantage, when it comes to the "abandon policy" strategy. If we put aside for a moment that the views of the American people have moved left and the Republican Party is now completely out of step with the voters, there is another aspect to this phenomenon. Often the Republican Party sees "not doing things" as something to be praised and revered. Many in the Republican Party value making government as small as possible, taking power away from the government, shuttering entire federal departments, and showing how little government can and should do. As a result, even pointing out that the Right is proposing nothing and doing nothing isn't effective because to many Republican voters, that's exactly what they want to see government do.

Historically, the Right's ideological inclination leans toward minimal government intervention in both the economic and personal spheres. The Republican Party has championed deregulation, a free market economy, and personal liberties, asserting that government is best when it governs least. This predilection is evident in the party's consistent push for tax cuts, the rollback of governmental regulations, and its desire to dismantle or shrink government agencies and programs, often including but not limited to the Department of Education, the Department of Energy, the Department of Commerce, the FBI, the IRS, and numerous others. The GOP's affinity for "not doing things" isn't a recent deviation; it's a foundational principle.

The Right often frames their reluctance to pass expansive policies or allocate extensive resources as fiscal prudence. By equating government spending with fiscal irresponsibility, they have positioned themselves as the guardians of the nation's purse strings. This narrative, however well it resonates with their base, ignores the nuance that not all government spending is bad and that investments in infrastructure, education, and health can lead to long-term economic benefits.

As frustrating as it is to see one party abandon policy and propose nothing of value, it's more frustrating to see that strategy win them elections, and unless the Democratic Party and the American Left figure out how to run against such a strategy, there's no reason for Republicans to come back to policy.

The solution comes in two parts, one more structural and systemic, the other more related to specific campaigns.

Rachel Bitecofer, a political scientist and frequent guest on *The David Pakman Show*, has weighed in on this situation, telling *Salon* in a November 2021 interview that Democrats must "redesign how they run election campaigns to build on the realities of the electorate and the impact of polarization and hyper-partisanship."[18] In other words, Democrats must run elections based on the electorate that exists, not the electorate that the Democratic Party wishes existed. This is the short-term approach.

At the campaign level, sounding like a broken record, candidates running against Republicans must make clear that the cultural issues and fear-mongering are meant to distract voters from the undeniable truth that these very Republicans aren't even claiming that they will accomplish anything realistic, and their few promises are truly impossibilities, in the style of Trump's plan to "build a wall with Mexico that Mexico will pay for," or to replace Obamacare with a "beautiful plan" that will cost less, be better, and cover everyone. Even to those whose view is that the government should do very little, it should be made clear that Republicans aren't promising anything because they truly don't plan to do anything. This approach is seen as a virtue for the Right, which believes government *should not* do much, if anything, unless it benefits their agenda. Instead they are using their positions of power to enrich themselves and gain power for power's sake. To combat Republican candidates at the more tactical level, Democratic campaigns should employ the following methods.

MAINTAINING MESSAGE DISCIPLINE AND CONSISTENCY

When Republicans capitalize on cultural issues and avoid real policy, Democrats must counter with a unified and consistent message. By hammering home the point that their opponents lack a concrete policy plan, Democrats can force Republicans to defend their lack of vision. Every interview, town hall, and debate provide an opportunity to reinforce this

narrative and highlight the lack of substance among their political opponents. In speeches, campaign ads, and debates, the contrast must be made.

During debates and public engagements, Democratic candidates
should be equipped with instant fact-checks to point out when a Republican opponent diverts to culture wars instead of policy. This could be
followed by a prompt question: "But what's your policy on this?"

HIGHLIGHTING THE CONSEQUENCES OF INACTION

Use ad campaigns to show the real-world consequences of having
representatives with no policy plans. Illustrate scenarios where a lack of
policy leads to stagnation, unemployment, or other issues. Countless examples exist where inaction on a budget, health care, or education led to
tangible and real disasters and tragedies. There is no shortage.

Highlight previous instances where Republican promises such as the
"beautiful health-care plan" were never realized. Emphasize that not having a policy isn't just about the future—it's a pattern of inaction.

ENGAGING AND EDUCATING

There may be a temptation to dismiss certain sections of the electorate as unreachable, but this is ill-advised in the long-term sense. In
the short term, I've acknowledged the apparent futility of arguing with
the most extreme MAGA-type cult members as a campaign strategy, particularly when encouraging like-minded nonvoters to vote is a far more
productive tactic. However, in the bigger picture across entire campaigns,
Democrats should be on the ground, engaging with voters, and demysti-
fying their policies to those across the political spectrum.

On the structural side, thinking more long term, the solution is a more
educated electorate, which leads us back to our chapter on critical thinking. A more informed electorate that is able to think for itself is less likely
to fall for the sophistry and fluff of the fact- and policy-free Republican
approach. There is a reason that Republicans have fought for decades
against properly funding public education, and against teaching critical
thinking, philosophy, and media literacy to young kids. Such education
would create more educated individuals who are less likely to fall for

their brand of politics in the first place. The more strategic long-term approaches here will not be unique to solving this problem and will remind readers of previous chapters, at least in part. Some ideas include the following approaches.

STRENGTHENING PUBLIC EDUCATION

Given the Republicans' resistance to funding public education adequately, Democrats can champion this cause. A populace that is educated from a young age is better equipped to discern substance from fluff. Push for curriculum reforms that make students more civic-minded and aware of the political landscape.

EXPLAINING THE CONNECTION BETWEEN ELECTED OFFICIALS AND REAL-WORLD CIRCUMSTANCES

From my experiences speaking to voters in all areas of the political spectrum, it is a common occurrence that voters will not directly connect how their votes influence their circumstances. During the 2024 Republican primary, we saw many examples of voters, angry with President Joe Biden, paradoxically explaining that thanks to the VA or Medicare, they had health insurance.[19] This example is emblematic of the problem, wherein voters ideologically believe that they are aligned with, in this case, Donald Trump rather than Joe Biden, but are praising social programs that Biden has sought to strengthen, while Trump showed indifference to or even disdain for those programs. Understanding the direct connection between votes and their lives will benefit the Left.

INTRODUCING CRITICAL THINKING AND MEDIA LITERACY SOONER

The earlier that children are exposed to critical thinking exercises, the more adept they become at recognizing and challenging baseless arguments. Introduce problem-solving, debate, and logic courses at middle-school levels. Given the era of misinformation we live in, media literacy should be a cornerstone of the curriculum. Workshops, seminars, and courses that teach students to differentiate between credible and non-credible sources can arm them against propaganda.

The emergence of a major political party that forgoes policy in favor of cultural issues and emotionally driven rhetoric may seem like a passing phase, but the political shifts of the past few years suggest it may be a longer-term phenomenon, especially if the Left and clear-thinking rational people do nothing to push back against it. Fighting against a party that operates on emotion rather than substance requires both tactical sense and a strategic overhaul. It demands that Democrats and the broader Left not only highlight the void of policy from the Right but also champion their own policies with vigor and clarity.

This is a serious challenge. Simple solutions and catchy slogans under the umbrella of populist rhetoric delivered by a charismatic strongman are enticing, especially in an era of bite-sized information and relentless news cycles. The goal is clear: to create an electorate that demands substance, that won't be swayed by the loudest voice but by the most credible. A nation that values substance over showmanship will naturally sideline those who offer nothing but smoke and mirrors. It's not clear that at this time the American electorate in sum total is on the side of substance, and to some degree it is not through any fault of their own. The future of American politics must be a return to policy, to substance, and to meaningful debates about the path forward. The responsibility of steering it in that direction falls on every informed citizen, every educator, and every genuine public servant.

CHAPTER 7

WHY DOES THE RIGHT
KEEP WINNING?

Despite public opinion continuing to shift steadily in the direction of progressive values on countless issues, the Republican Party remains a viable and even successful political party in the United States. Americans are increasingly in agreement with leftist positions on issues including abortion, a government's responsibility to provide a basic level of health care to everyone, progressive taxation of the very rich, our responsibility to the environment, and many others, yet Republicans regularly win elections. What explains this apparent incongruity? The central paradox at play is almost inconceivable: while voters continue moving to the left in the United States on policy, the Republican Party continues to win by moving further to the right.

The answer has three components: The Republican Party (1) is better at campaigning, (2) benefits from gerrymandering and the urban/rural systemic divide, and (3) is extraordinarily successful at using contrived cultural issues to raise disproportionately more money, or to avoid serious discussions of policy that would be exposed as totally absent from their platforms. We'll look at each of these in turn. In addition, there is a fundamental lack of "democracy" in our democracy; certain institutions and policies are fundamentally antidemocratic.

When it comes to campaigning, Republicans have more effectively understood and capitalized on the areas of focus that bring their voters to the polls. At the national level during the Trump era, with the GOP's failures in the 2018, 2020, and 2022 elections, this has started to change, but the broader analysis, including at the local level, remains disturbingly accurate. Gun safety regulations are an instructive example. Putting gun safety regulations front and center in a campaign hurts Democrats, or the more left-leaning candidate within a Republican primary. Although most Democratic voters favor a number of often-proposed gun safety regulations, those individuals already plan to vote even without gun safety becoming an issue. On the other hand, Democrats or centrist Republicans who choose to play up gun safety regulation provide the perfect impetus for Republican candidates to fearmonger around candidates who will "take your guns," ultimately motivating their side more than the Democratic electorate. This is a self-inflicted error from many Democrats.

Republicans are particularly good at weaponizing cultural issues to win elections, even fabricated cultural issues often supported by outright demonstrable lies. The 2021 Virginia gubernatorial election is a great example of both errors by Democrats and shrewd—but dishonest—tactics from Republicans. Republican Glenn Youngkin, without distancing himself from former president Donald Trump or embracing him, ran a campaign focused on "fixing" education, premised on the false notion that he would stop the teaching of critical race theory (CRT) in Virginia schools. In reality, CRT was not being taught in Virginia schools, but it was the flavor of the month at the time for a Republican Party running very low on policy ideas. Meanwhile, Democratic candidate Terry McAuliffe made the mistake of running against Donald Trump in the sense of running against "Trumpism," despite Youngkin never truly embracing Trump. What could have been an important win for the Democratic Party became a powerful victory for the Republican Party when Youngkin defeated McAuliffe in November 2021.

Political strategist and analyst Rachel Bitecofer has written about and discussed with me during numerous interviews the specific techniques used by the American right wing. She says that because "Americans are not particularly civic-minded or engaged" and Democrats "tend to have an idealized version of voters" who "want a very wonky, policy-based discussion," they end up leaving the door wide open for Republicans to use cultural issues and fear-based emotion to win elections. This works, Bitecofer says, because people are "better motivated by emotions," but also because it's easier to convince people who are less interested in politics with such fear-based emotional appeals.

Taking this framework into account, McAuliffe would have been far better served focusing his campaign on issues that voters indicated matter to them. Most voters support raising the top tax rate on the richest Americans. At the time, most voters supported the then-proposed Biden spending plan of $3.5 trillion.[1] Economic issues continued to reign supreme in polling both nationally and in Virginia. However, McAuliffe failed to really focus on those practical issues, instead fighting—but with the wrong tactics—over the cultural and superficial issues. McAuliffe's attacks on Youngkin as too aligned with Trump failed to land, but more importantly failed to motivate Democratic-leaning voters to get out and vote. McAuliffe also made strategic mistakes in fighting Youngkin on cultural issues, flippantly saying about critical race theory during a campaign debate, "I don't think parents should be telling schools what they should teach," which was repeated on a loop going into the final days of the campaign.[2] Instead, it likely would have been more effective to state that critical race theory is a fringe issue meant to divide voters, and that in fact there are no K-12 schools in Virginia teaching CRT anyway.

Another critical element of this advantage on campaigning comes from the borderline instantaneous way in which the Republican Party will feed the echo machine and immediately and nearly unanimously get on message and focus on a particular storyline about an issue. During the Senate confirmation hearings for then-future Supreme Court justice Ketanji Brown Jackson, Republican senator Josh Hawley began a narrative about Jackson being "soft on child pornography offenders" based on a handful of sentences handed out among many in a long history of sentencing on issues surrounding explicit sexual images of children.[3] The claim was baseless—when taken in context, her sentencing on these cases sat right around sentencing from other judges, and was completely unremarkable—but by the next day, other Republican legislators including Elise Stefanik cosigned a letter saying Jackson was soft on child porn, and it quickly became a lead story and theme of her confirmation hearings and the coverage thereof.

As a brief aside, many sensible progressives would agree that the way race- and gender-related issues are taught in the United States can be, at minimum, clumsy, and could use some modification. Unfortunately, the

American right wing, despite their focus on these issues, has become a steadfast impediment to such reform by failing to offer anything approximating an intelligent critique.

These examples should also underscore a broader, more fundamental theme: Republicans have been exceedingly proficient at distilling complex, multifaceted issues into simple, emotive narratives that resonate with their base. Another illustrative instance is the portrayal of movements like "defund the police." Democrats who supported calls to reform police rarely actually supported defunding the police. They were predominantly advocating for nuanced policy adjustments such as reallocating funds to other critical public services, adding a mental health component to police training, creating alternative first responders trained in mental health to respond to certain calls, and other similar reforms. Republicans successfully manipulated the movement to claim that Democrats overall want to defund and end police departments in a way that suggested a penchant for a total abandonment of law and order, thereby sparking fear and opposition among many voters who might otherwise be receptive to police reform. Consequently, Democrats find themselves ensnared in a web of misinformation, compelled to defend policies that were never actually proposed, and hence struggling to communicate their authentic policy intentions to the electorate.

Republicans also benefit from gerrymandering and the urban/rural divide that is the result of politico-cultural differences. Because Republicans have controlled the mechanisms for drawing districts in so many states for so long, they've built an advantage on the basis of gerrymandering alone. In addition to this, there are cultural realities in the United States in which, on average, left-leaning voters are more likely to live in cities and urban areas, while right-leaning voters are more likely to live more rurally. The combination of these two factors gives Republicans an edge, which, in the 2018 midterm congressional election, required Democrats to win the popular vote by an 11 point margin in order to win a majority in the US House.[4] This is a result of congressional district gerrymandering that creates overwhelmingly blue districts where victory margins are large for Democrats, taking Democratic voters away from what could be many competitive districts. Getting 50 percent of the vote for Democrats leads to having fewer than 50 percent of the seats due to much of that vote total being overwhelming victories in dark blue counties where there are large margins of victory.

Conversely, the way districts are designed often ends up diffusing Democratic votes across numerous constituencies, thereby weakening their overall impact in electoral outcomes. The urban/rural divide plays into this disadvantage. Democrats tend to concentrate in urban environments where their votes are "wasted" in secure seats, while Republicans are spread out in a way that maximizes their electoral advantage across numerous districts. This geographical distribution creates an inadvertent systemic bias. While left-leaning policies might be celebrated in densely populated urban areas, their impact on policymaking is curtailed by a system that affords disproportionate representation to less populated, rural areas. The US Senate and the Electoral College are prime examples of how this urban/rural split amplifies the political influence of sparsely populated regions. As a result, to win half of congressional seats, Democrats need to get a majority of the votes in many deliberately competitive districts, and by definition, their easy victories in the most gerrymandered blue districts will pile onto their vote total, leaving them with half of the seats at 54 percent of the total vote.

The urban/rural divide is not only a matter of geography but also manifests as yet another deep-seated politico-cultural divide. Urban environments, with their dense, diverse populations and exposure to global flows of people and ideas, tend to harbor progressive values, thus aligning more closely with Democratic platforms. Rural areas, on the other hand, often uphold traditional, conservative values, leading to a steadfast alignment with the Republican Party. It's not merely a matter of ideological disagreement; this divide is perpetuated and exacerbated by different lived experiences, economic priorities, and social environments between urban and rural dwellers. The urban voter is often more concerned with issues like public transportation, affordable housing, and social services, whereas the rural voter may prioritize agricultural policy, Second Amendment rights, and conservative social values.

The way that the political landscape has evolved has also led to Republicans amplifying the urban/rural divide, strategically utilizing it to generate a "them versus us" narrative that is often part of the earlier discussed populist rhetoric and a calling card of the MAGA wing of the Republican

Party. Republicans have adeptly portrayed themselves as the champions of "real" America, defending traditional values and ways of life against the perceived onslaught of liberal, urban elites. This narrative, although simplistic and divisive, has proven politically potent, rallying support in key electoral areas and providing the GOP with a robust and reliable voter base, even in the face of shifting national demographics and values.

These systemic and cultural factors, both deliberate and incidental, interact to create an electoral environment where the Democratic Party, despite often securing a larger share of the popular vote, faces an uphill battle in translating this support into tangible political power and policy implementation. In turn, this perpetuates a political arena wherein the Republican Party, despite needing to appeal to a narrower demographic, continues to exert a substantial, sometimes disproportionate, influence on the American political and legislative landscape. Moving forward, understanding and addressing these dynamics will be pivotal for Democrats if they are to effectively navigate this skewed electoral terrain and translate widespread voter support into meaningful political victories.

Next is the issue of contrived cultural issues alluded to in our section on Republicans being better at campaigning. Despite national opinion on many social issues moving more to the left over the last forty years, the conservative viewpoints on these very issues remain an effective method for raising money. Since *Roe v. Wade* was decided by the Supreme Court in 1973, there has never been more support for abortion being legal in most cases than there is now. However, anti-choice groups, including evangelical Christians, continue to raise massive amounts of money for anti-abortion candidates. Despite being increasingly out of step with the national opinion on abortion, it's a tremendously effective way to raise money, and the candidate who raises the most money tends to win in American politics. Ultimately, thanks to the Supreme Court's shift to the right over time, cemented by the three justices nominated by President Donald Trump, *Roe v. Wade* was reversed.

Similarly, long after gay marriage was legalized nationally in the United States by the Supreme Court's 2015 decision in *Obergefell v. Hodges*, anti-LGBTQ+ groups and candidates continued raising vast sums of money, initially to send candidates to Washington to "fight gay marriage." Once it became evident that legal gay marriage was the law of the land, the focus shifted to fighting against LGBTQ+ rights on the basis of so-called religious freedom to discriminate against queer individuals as employees or customers or in other ways. Polling shows that Americans are more in favor than ever of legal gay marriage, yet it continues to be a fundraising boon for the most extreme elements of the Republican Party.

Not to be ignored in this context of Republican policy being at odds with the interests of Republican voters is the phenomenon that took place during the COVID-19 pandemic in the United States. Vaccination in the United States became highly partisan, with high COVID vaccination rates and adherence to public health guidelines among those on the political left and most in the center contrasted with stunningly low vaccine adoption by Republican voters and, in particular, supporters of Donald Trump. As a result of this partisan vaccination and health guideline gap, COVID case rates were dramatically higher in Republican voting states. At the county level, higher Trump support correlated directly with higher COVID case rates, hospitalization rates, and death rates. Republicans disproportionately were dying of COVID as a result, in part, of their lower vaccination rates and more limited adherence to public health guidelines.

Another salient example involves the controversy surrounding former NFL football player Colin Kaepernick and the wider NFL protests. When Kaepernick began kneeling during the national anthem to protest racial injustice and police brutality, it sparked widespread debate and division across the nation. The Republican Party, particularly under the Trump administration, was swift to hijack the narrative, transforming a protest against racial injustice into a purported affront against the military and the nation. The framing of this issue was crafted by the right wing to evoke fervent nationalism and indignation among conservative voters, despite the protesters' explicit clarification that their actions were not intended to disrespect the military. This divisive issue was skillfully utilized by the Republicans to galvanize their base, raise funds, and portray themselves as staunch defenders of patriotic values, even when the primary issue at hand—racial injustice—was left unaddressed.

Another provocative issue has been the discourse surrounding transgender rights, particularly in the realm of sports. A number of Republican-led states have pursued or enacted legislation that bans transgender women and girls from competing in sports consistent with their gender identity. This is despite widespread criticism and evidence suggesting that such policies are not only discriminatory but also based on misrepresented and selectively interpreted science.[5] By stoking fears and prejudices related to the so-called fairness in women's sports and the integrity of single-sex spaces, the Republican Party was able to mobilize and entrench support among conservative voters, even when such policies were frequently at odds with the principles of equality and inclusivity.

In all of these examples, it's evident that the contrived or manipulated cultural issues did not merely serve to define policy directions but were instrumental in constructing potent electoral narratives that facilitated fundraising, mobilized voter bases, and crafted a cohesive, albeit frequently misleading, message. These instances underscore the adept utilization of sociocultural issues by the Republicans to navigate the electoral landscape, often prioritizing electoral gain over policy substance and ethical considerations.

Having reviewed areas in which Republicans have generated an advantage for themselves, we also must address areas of our elections and the legislative branch of government that are fundamentally antidemocratic. We will consider the Electoral College, which was covered earlier, the filibuster, the US Senate, and voter suppression tactics. There are structures and mechanisms in place that, while arguably integral to the functioning of the nation, have been manipulated or leveraged in ways that can subvert the democratic ethos they were built on. For Republicans, some of these structures and mechanisms have been wielded to sustain and consolidate power, often misaligning with the principle of representative democracy.

THE ELECTORAL COLLEGE

The Electoral College is undeniably an institution that can and often does subvert the popular vote, to the advantage of Republicans. The Electoral College system, in place since the US Constitution's ratification, was designed as a compromise between those who wanted the president to be elected directly by the people and those who preferred that Congress select the president. While the system was intended to serve as a buffer against potential populist influences and to ensure the voices of smaller states were heard, it is inherently antidemocratic in a number of ways.

Most states employ a "winner-takes-all" method, where the candidate receiving the majority of the popular vote gets all of that state's electoral votes. This system means that a person's vote might not be represented in the final electoral tally if they supported the losing candidate in their state. A candidate could win 49 percent of the vote in just about every state and end up with close to zero electoral votes.

Because every state is guaranteed at least three electoral votes (representing two senators and at least one representative), states with smaller populations have a disproportionate influence in the Electoral College. For instance, while California might have one electoral vote for every 712,000 people, Wyoming has one for every 195,000. This discrepancy means a citizen's vote cast in Wyoming has over 3.5 times more influence in determining the president than a vote cast in California.[6]

The victories of George W. Bush in 2000 and Donald Trump in 2016, despite losing the popular vote, spotlight the skewed nature of this system. In these instances, by focusing campaigns on key swing states and leveraging the winner-takes-all approach most states employ in assigning electoral votes, the Republican Party has managed to secure presidential victories even in the face of popular vote losses. In some cases, as in 2020, that margin of defeat in the popular vote is significant.

To abolish the Electoral College would require a constitutional amendment. This is a challenging process that needs a two-thirds majority in both the House of Representatives and the Senate, followed by ratification by three-fourths of the state legislatures or conventions. Given the inherent advantages the system offers to less populated states, it's questionable whether enough states would ever support such an amendment.

Recognizing the difficulty of amending the Constitution, some have proposed the National Popular Vote Interstate Compact (NPVIC) as a workaround. This is an agreement among participating states to award all their respective electoral votes to the presidential candidate who wins the overall national popular vote, regardless of the individual state results. For example, if Pennsylvania joined the agreement, Pennsylvania's electoral votes would be given to whichever candidate wins the national popular vote, regardless of who receives more votes in Pennsylvania. This is allowed because states have significant discretion in how they allocate their Electoral College votes. The US Constitution gives states the power to determine the manner in which their electors are chosen.

For the compact to take effect, states representing at least 270 electoral votes (the minimum required to win the presidency) must join. As of this writing, the NPVIC has been enacted by seventeen states totaling 205 electoral votes.[7] While the concept behind the NPVIC is constitutionally sound based on the states' power to determine elector allocation, the compact could face legal challenges. Some have raised concerns about whether the compact would need approval from Congress under the Compact Clause of the Constitution. Others suggest it could face challenges based on the argument that it disrupts the federal balance of power.

THE FILIBUSTER

Senate rules allow for a legislative procedure that permits individual senators to extend debate on a piece of legislation, effectively preventing or delaying its passage. Called the "filibuster," the term originates from a Dutch word meaning "pirate," reflecting its use as a tool to "hold hostage" the legislative process.

Originally, the filibuster involved senators taking the floor and actually speaking for an extended period of time—a "talking filibuster"—on any topic they wished, holding the Senate's attention and preventing a vote on the bill in question. Famous instances include Senator Strom Thurmond's 1957 speech lasting over twenty-four hours in opposition to the Civil Rights Act.

To end a filibuster and bring a bill to a vote, the Senate can invoke a "cloture" motion. This requires a three-fifths majority (typically sixty out of one hundred senators). If the motion is successful, the filibustering senator(s) can no longer block the bill from coming to a vote.

More recently, the process has evolved. Rather than physically holding the floor and speaking for hours, senators can simply indicate their intent to filibuster, which then requires the aforementioned sixty-vote threshold to proceed. This has made the filibuster a more common and potent tool for obstruction, as the mere threat of a filibuster can be enough to stall legislation without the need for extended speeches.

The filibuster, though not exclusively exploited by Republicans, has been notably utilized to stymie legislative processes and inhibit the passage of laws, even those with broad public and bipartisan support. Notably, the persistent use of the filibuster has allowed a Senate minority to prevent or delay crucial legislation on issues such as gun control, immigration reform, and voting rights, thereby undermining majority rule and perpetuating legislative gridlock.

The continued existence of the filibuster is not without disagreement today. Critics argue it gives a minority of senators disproportionate power, allowing them to block legislation even when it has majority support. They also claim it contributes to legislative gridlock and hinders the Senate's ability to function efficiently. Proponents maintain that the filibuster is essential to protect the rights of the minority and encourage bipartisan cooperation by requiring a supermajority for contentious issues.

Over the years, some reforms such as the cloture rule have aimed to curb the power of the filibuster. More recently, the Senate has seen changes to the filibuster rules as they apply to certain nominations. For instance, in 2013 and 2017, the rules were changed to allow for a simple majority vote for executive and judicial nominations, excluding those to the Supreme Court. However, the broader debate about the role and future of the filibuster in the Senate continues.

THE US SENATE

The US Senate is an undemocratic body by design in that regardless of a state's population, each state has two senators. Smaller, typically more conservative states wield disproportionate power relative to their population. Wyoming, with a population of approximately 580,000, has the same Senate representation as California, with a population over 39 million. This structural incongruence has allowed Republicans to maintain a strong, sometimes dominant, presence in the Senate, enabling them to wield significant legislative and judicial appointment power, even when representing a minority of the American population. As a result, Republicans can control more than half of the Senate seats with senators representing a minority of the US population.

Now that we understand the filibuster, the US Senate's antidemocratic nature becomes even more pronounced. Even a US Senate with fifty-nine Democrats and forty-one Republicans, in which the forty-one Republicans represent well under 50 percent of the US population, can use the filibuster to obstruct all kinds of crucial legislation.

The Senate has the exclusive authority to confirm or reject presidential appointments to the executive and judicial branches, including lifetime appointments to the US Supreme Court. This authority can significantly influence the balance of power, and decisions made by a Senate representing a minority of the population can have long-lasting implications. A multitude of judges can be confirmed to lifetime jobs by the senators representing a minority of the American population.

The Senate also has the power to ratify international treaties, which requires a two-thirds majority. A minority of senators can thus block treaties supported by a majority of both the Senate and the broader US population.

The lack of democracy in the Senate becomes even more pronounced when one considers the influence of money in Senate races, which is particularly noteworthy due to the high costs of statewide campaigns. Wealthy donors, political action committees (PACs), and super PACs can exert significant influence, which some argue dilutes the democratic principle of "one person, one vote." When layered onto the already antidemocratic Senate, a small number of donors, by influencing just a few races, can get Republicans to over fifty seats in the Senate, therefore allowing Republicans to control the legislative body on the basis of seats that represent well short of 50 percent of the US population.

VOTER SUPPRESSION

Voter suppression has emerged as a particularly contentious and decidedly antidemocratic tactic, with numerous instances where Republican-led states implemented policies that make accessing the vote more difficult, particularly for minority and lower-income communities. Measures such as stringent voter ID laws, purging of voter rolls, and reduction of polling places have been strategically utilized in various states to inhibit specific demographics from voting, under the often-debunked guise of preventing voter fraud. The 2013 Supreme Court decision in *Shelby County v. Holder*, which invalidated a critical component of the Voting Rights Act, has given states more latitude in implementing these restrictive voting measures without federal scrutiny or pre-clearance.

As discussed earlier, requiring identification to vote might sound reasonable on the surface, but not all voters have easy access to identification.

Some citizens, especially the elderly, may not have been born in a hospital and thus may not have a birth certificate, a requirement to obtain a government-issued ID. These laws disproportionately impact minority voters, students, and the elderly. The paperwork required to get a "free" voter ID can be costly.

Some states have been known to aggressively purge their voter rolls, claiming to update them. However, these purges often remove eligible voters. In some cases, voters aren't notified and only discover they've been purged when they turn up at the polls.

Early voting allows citizens to cast their ballots in person on a day other than Election Day. However, some states have cut back on the number of days allowed for early voting, which particularly affects workers who can't afford to take time off on a Tuesday to vote. Especially relevant during the COVID-19 pandemic, some states made it harder to vote by mail, despite the health risks of in-person voting.

In some areas, especially in minority communities, polling places have been closed or relocated, making them less accessible. This often results in longer lines and waiting times, discouraging some people from voting. Many states strip citizens of their voting rights if they have felony convictions. While some states restore voting rights once a person has completed their sentence, others continue to deny the vote to people with past convictions, sometimes for life.

Some states have imposed strict rules about who can register voters, and when and how registrations can take place. This can make it harder for new voters, especially younger ones or those from marginalized communities, to get registered. Some voters face intimidation at the polls, ranging from aggressive questioning to threats of violence. There have also been campaigns of misinformation, where voters are given incorrect details about when and where to vote, or false information about the requirements.

Proponents of many of these measures argue that they are necessary to prevent voter fraud. However, numerous studies have shown that voter fraud is extremely rare in the US, and many of these measures disproportionately impact minority, elderly, and low-income voters. In reality, when people do get caught committing voter fraud at the individual level, it has in more recent history, more often than not, been Trump-supporting Republicans, who simultaneously claim that it is Democrats who commit this type of fraud.[8]

These antidemocratic facets allow for a potent strategy that has enabled the Republican Party to secure and maintain political power, often misaligned with the will of the majority. The consequential misrepresentation and institutional hurdles foster an environment where policies and judicial appointments often do not reflect the desires and needs of the broader American populace.

We have taken a brief tour through the most important factors contributing to a Republican Party that continues to win, despite many reasons why it should be losing. Republicans are generally better at campaigning, especially at the local and state levels. They have the structural advantages in national campaigns of gerrymandering, and also have leveraged contrived social and cultural issues that have become media flashpoints to replace the total lack of policy, many of which have become the opposite of majority American opinion. Beyond this, there are also antidemocratic elements in our system, including the Electoral College and US Senate, which further help Republicans. Lastly, Republicans have also fought to make voting harder through a variety of voter suppression tactics.

Navigating this labyrinth, we've uncovered the sly maneuvers, built-in biases, and relics of history that have given the GOP an upper hand at the structural level. While their mastery is begrudgingly admirable, it raises the question: At what cost? As the world watches, the bedrock principles of American democracy have wobbled more since the Trump era than at any other time in modern political history.

So then, what next? While we can dissect the tactics and strategies, lament about systemic flaws, and rail against the unfairness of the post-truth environment created by the Right, we also need to be pragmatic. Facing a system that's loaded with traps and pitfalls, how should one play the game? Dive headfirst, hoping for massive upheaval, or make savvy, measured moves that inch us toward a better future? As we pivot to our next chapter, we'll tackle the question of consuming media. When should the Left double down, and when should we accept smaller yet guaranteed wins?

CHAPTER 8

HOW TO (RESPONSIBLY) CONSUME MEDIA

The media has long been referred to as the "fourth estate" of government. It is supposed to serve as a watchdog, a check on power, and a platform for public discourse. Yet its symbiotic relationship with power and money and its impact on critical thinking and the health of democracy are multifaceted. On one hand, media informs the public, but on the other, it can influence perceptions and, intentionally or unintentionally, shape political narratives. As a result, every political issue, every issue of concern to activists, and any area of interest to grassroots activism efforts will be mediated and impacted by the media system and coverage by media of that issue.

The media plays a pivotal role in the life cycle of activist movements. It can amplify the voices of grassroots campaigns, drawing attention to underrepresented issues and communities. Conversely, it can also overshadow or misrepresent these movements, either by misconstruing their aims or by focusing on sensationalist elements. Effective activism and resistance to a post-truth America in the modern age require an understanding of the media landscape. Knowing how to harness media attention, navigate its pitfalls, and leverage its platforms is crucial for activists. In essence, media doesn't just report on activism; it shapes and mediates its outcomes in the broader public sphere.

Going back to the earliest days of the country, newspapers were the primary medium through which political leaders communicated with the public. Partisanship was overt; newspapers openly endorsed candidates and took sides on issues. With the advent of radio and television, political messaging transformed. Broadcasters such as Edward R. Murrow and Walter Cronkite became trusted figures, delivering news to living rooms across the country. The twenty-four-hour news cycle, born from cable news, amplified the immediacy and intensity of political coverage. Now in the digital age, social media platforms and online news have further democratized information dissemination but also fragmented sources and increased the spread of misinformation. Media impacts politics and activism in a number of ways, some of which are listed below.

MEDIA BIAS

Accusations of media bias are not new, but they've gained significant traction in recent decades. Critics argue that certain networks or publications skew their coverage to favor specific political ideologies, leading to a polarized and misinformed public. Studies have shown that media consumption can indeed shape political perceptions. For instance, viewers of distinctly left- or right-leaning outlets are more likely to have stronger partisan views.[1] Furthermore, the rise of echo chambers on platforms like Facebook and X means individuals are often exposed to a narrow range of perspectives, reinforcing preexisting beliefs.

MEDIA INFLUENCE THROUGH ADVERTISING

Corporate and lobbying influence: Advertising is a significant revenue source for media outlets. Corporations, special interest groups, and lobbyists spend vast sums to push specific narratives or interests through advertising. This commercial pressure can influence the stance of media entities, leading to potential conflicts of interest where news might be presented in ways favorable to these advertisers. Even without directly influencing the positions of the reporters or channels, the presence of such influence campaigns during commercial breaks and in sponsored segments can still have a massive impact on political outcomes.

Political advertising: Come election season, political advertisements flood the media. These ads, often funded by super PACs and dark money groups, aim to shape public opinion for or against particular candidates or issues. The financial power behind such advertising campaigns can distort genuine public discourse, emphasizing well-funded narratives over grass-roots concerns.

MEDIA'S ROLE IN ELECTIONS

The media's influence becomes most evident during election cycles. Endorsements from prominent publications can boost a candidate's credibility. However, the disparity in coverage can also tilt the scales. A candidate receiving a substantial amount of attention, whether positive or negative, can overshadow others, dictating the flow of the campaign. The 2016 US presidential election was a notable example, where disproportionate media focus on specific candidates and issues arguably influenced voter perceptions and choices.[2]

The challenge ultimately lies in ensuring these biases don't eclipse the broader, necessary discourse. The nexus of media, money, and politics is intricate, but understanding this relationship is vital for activists and informed citizens. The aim should be a media environment where core issues and grassroots concerns are given as much attention as well-funded narratives and sensationalistic stories.

Ideas for reform in the media space are numerous. Government-sponsored public media outlets, free from the pressure of advertising revenues, can offer a less overtly biased perspective. With proper checks and balances, public media can serve as a counterbalance to commercial outlets that may be influenced by advertisers or corporate interests. Equipping voters and activists with the tools to critically assess the information they consume is essential. This includes understanding the sources of news, identifying bias, and discerning between genuine news and misinformation. Transparency in advertising, through mandating clear disclosures in political and issue-based advertising, would also help. Moreover, when it comes to social media platforms, clear labeling of sponsored content and political ads and disclosure of funding sources would help to combat the spread of misinformation. Lastly, encouraging more diverse media ownership to counteract the media monopolies and concentration of media ownership that leads to a lack of diversity in news perspectives should be supported by government. Regulations that promote diverse media ownership can ensure a multiplicity of voices in the media landscape.

Consuming and creating news, particularly in an engaged and empathetic way, can be notably stressful and depressing. On a planet of nearly eight billion people, and in a country of more than 330 million people, there are horrible events taking place daily, making it difficult to remain even remotely optimistic about the future. As a result, making deliberate choices about news consumption and curation of sources as a news creator, and maintaining balance and perspective, are important decisions to be made by any media consumer. There is also ongoing debate over whether it is ethical to provide a platform to extreme, radical voices. This debate, which I've found myself at the center of for more than a decade, often becomes a Manichean argument between black-and-white extremes. The more sensible approach is the idea of responsible platforming; bad ideas notable enough to warrant refutation should be platformed by those capable and prepared to refute and expose them as bad ideas. We will explore both sides of this in this chapter, from the perspective of news consumer and news creator.

At the core, it's important to understand the systemic realities that impact what becomes news. This is a topic not often given thought, but it is fundamental. Every day, a massive number of events take place: births, deaths, accidents, elections, legislative occurrences, bankruptcies, companies going public, scientific discoveries, successful and unsuccessful medical procedures, fundraisers, sporting events, and the like. Yet only some of them become "news" in the sense of being reported on, and as individuals, we can only find out about a fraction of those news items, and truly understand or think about a smaller portion therein.

The structure of news is the primary determinant of the selection that takes place. In talking about corporate for-profit news, there is a bias to sensationalism that is a primary filter for what becomes news, and negative events are more likely to meet the sensationalist criteria than positive events, so this will skew corporate news toward the negative. Subsequently, because corporate news is primarily funded by advertisers, news items will tend to be skewed toward what is inoffensive to the media entity's advertisers. Lastly, news items will also be chosen based on convenience and cost. For example, if a corporate media outlet has a reporter at the White House every day, but not at a water treatment plant or public library, they will, on average, report more often from the White House, even on days when there may be sensational news that would be acceptable to advertisers coming from the water treatment plant or public library.

This is a regular balancing act. As many of us are all too aware, if an event is sensational enough, it will supersede the other priorities, such as a mass shooting for example, or the BP Deepwater Horizon oil spill, which led to constant coverage of the event from near the location of the spill, despite BP being an advertiser on many media outlets, and media outlets not normally having reporters or camera crews near the location of the disaster.

Over time, for regular consumers of news, the effect of this corporate media bias can be both emotionally negative and deceiving in terms of what is happening in the world, and what the media's perspective on what is happening actually is. A more balanced and informative media outlet starts by making an analogy between news consumption and the food pyramid that was ubiquitous in school health classes in the United States for so long.

Foundational to the pyramid is epistemology and critical thinking, which is the basis of this book's argument. Moving up the pyramid, the next important ingredient is media literacy, followed by a host of liberal arts fields including history, philosophy, economics, sociology, and psychology. At the very top of the pyramid is news and current events.

Let's explore this pyramid in more detail.

The first step to being an informed news consumer is having a basis in epistemology (the study of knowledge) and critical thinking. That knowledge allows one to answer questions that include

- What is knowledge and what do I know?
- Why do I believe the things I believe?
- When is a belief justified?
- What are the limits of what can be known?
- How do I determine whether I'm evaluating a question correctly?
- Am I thinking in a logically consistent way?
- Are there logical fallacies at play?

Once this conceptual framework is in place, the next step on the pyramid is media literacy. Armed with a basis in epistemology and critical thinking, media literacy provides a powerful framework for evaluating and understanding media messages, including

- Who created this report/article/news show/podcast, and how does that affect its biases?
- What techniques are at play to attract my attention to this piece, including sensationalism, violence, fear, etc.?
- What perspectives are represented versus missing in this reporting?
- Is this a news or opinion piece? Could it be both, or deliberately unclear?
- Who paid for this, or how is it paid for, and how does that affect its bias?
- What action am I being encouraged to take, implicitly or explicitly, as a result of this news piece?
- What sources were used in the creation of this news piece?

It might appear as though once equipped with epistemology, critical thinking, and media literacy skills, one would be ready to start watching the news in a productive and informed manner, but in reality, our time is better spent, as a general rule, on an intermediate step, which is subject matter knowledge.

One can be well-versed in thinking skills and still end up uninformed, confused, or deceived by news if some basic subject matter knowledge is lacking. For this reason, to truly be informed news consumers of day-to-day events, it's ideal to have some basis in the general areas often covered by corporate media, including history, economics, sociology, psychology, medicine, science, and others.

This is clearly a significant amount of work. The important takeaway is that it need not all be done at once as a precursor to ever watching or listening to news. In an ideal scenario, thinking skills would start to be taught early in a child's life, in addition to the subject matter knowledge, so that these skills and knowledge both develop in concert with exposure to media messages.

To understand the importance of this knowledge pyramid, consider a topic as omnipresent as whether the US should get involved in a conflict in Latin America. Without the foundation proposed above, one would lack the historical knowledge of Latin American countries and American intervention in Latin America to truly evaluate what is taking place today. Without the media literacy skills, one would lack the ability to question and understand how the perspectives on American involvement in Latin America are directly shaped by the corporate entities doing the reporting. Without the critical thinking and epistemology framework, one would lack even the wherewithal to realize that these are questions that must be asked to really have an opportunity to meaningfully consume the news of the day.

A reasonable reaction would be to take time away from the news, given the intensity proposed, and that's the correct instinct. Part of maintaining a healthy relationship to news media is taking a break from the news. For me, during the intense production of a daily news and politics program, that has meant that when production is finished for the Friday episode, I watch no news and do not even engage in discussions about news and politics until the time comes to start preparing the Monday episode.

With regard to the platforming of extremists, while I was never particularly conspiratorial myself, nor personally susceptible to cults, I found quite appealing the idea of finding a "truth" that was both true and simple, much as we've discussed already in our chapter on critical thinking and in the subsequent chapter on ignoring policy and focusing only on simple principles. As one becomes educated, it is common to realize that the world is a complex adaptive system, and this often will naturally protect individuals from falling for extremism, cults, and radical thinking. As adults, we tend to realize that there are rarely simple explanations for anything but the most fundamental phenomena, and even then, simple outcomes often emerge from a very complex underlying infrastructure.

One of the appealing aspects of cults, conspiracy theories, and extremist beliefs is that they often provide easy, clear, simple explanations. In cults, it's the delightful simplicity that the cult leader knows all, and will tell you what is right, often based on knowledge the leader receives through direct contact with a higher power. This eliminates complexity and rescues followers from the need to sort things out for themselves. In conspiracy theories, a simple explanation for a horrible occurrence can feel much better than the realization that in such a complex system, bad things can happen for reasons that can't be predicted, and often for no discernible reason at all. It is far less unnerving to many to believe that a tragedy happened because it was planned and carried out rather than as the result of mere chance, odds, and timing. Extremist beliefs can provide the same false clarity in suggesting that the world's problems are the result of Jews, gays, Muslims, feminists, socialists, communists, people who believe in the science of vaccines, or people who accept the science of climate change.

Early in *The David Pakman Show*'s history, I began to interview extremists from varied organizations, including antigay churches, antisemitic political candidates, and others. The impetus to do these interviews was a desire to learn more about how one falls into such beliefs, whether the beliefs are resistant to reason, and on some basic level, whether those who hold such outrageous and vile beliefs appear to also be people able to engage in polite conversation. Reaction was swift and divided about such interviews. Most of my core audience understood the point of examining where extremism comes from—the extremists typically grew up in chaotic and broken homes—and also the point of pushing back against that extremism. However, some felt that interviewing and examining these individuals was platforming them such that they could spread their message, convert more people to their ideology or beliefs, and make the world a worse place.

Sometimes, the claim was that if I ignored them, they would simply go away, and interviewing them was what would allow their ideas to spread in the first place.

As is the case with the vast majority of issues in our world, the reality is not black-and-white. It is true that at least in theory, a listener might hear my interview with an antigay pastor and find their arguments so compelling that they would be convinced by their homophobic beliefs. It's conceptually possible that a viewer could watch my interview with an antisemitic conspiracy theorist and become a believer of those hateful ideas. At the same time, it's just as plausible that those already indoctrinated by those beliefs might see the promoters of their ideology fail or be humiliated in trying to explain those beliefs in such an interview with me, and end up deradicalized as a result. Anecdotally, hundreds of people have written to me over the years explaining that exactly this type of deradicalization took place as a result of content I created.

In sum total, the approach must be what I've called for years responsible platforming. In preparing for interviews with such extremists, I often watch previous interviews that have been done by other media outlets with the same person. Sometimes, the most vile and disgusting extremists will appear on other media outlets and receive absolutely no resistance whatsoever. I've seen hosts and news anchors treat them as if they were merely experts. This is irresponsible platforming and very well could lead to a viewer coming away with the impression that the extreme views are compelling and reasonable, or even that the interviewer agrees with those very views.

Another iteration is that hosts and interviewers will sometimes become so visibly furious during interviews with extremists that the entire exercise ends up serving no purpose whatsoever. This can backfire insofar as it can make the extremist appear to be the less unhinged of the two participants. This is more counterproductive than it is irresponsible, but it should still be avoided.

John Herrman asked in the *New York Times* in 2016, "Who's responsible when extremists get a platform?"[3] The article raises good questions about the types of content that are worthy of publication, who the decision makers should be and how those decisions should be made, and whether there is liability for publishing extremist content or ideas.

Herrman explores the implicit meaning of the word "platform" as a verb, as in "to platform" someone. Referring to a statement from former Trump propagandist Stephen K. Bannon, Herrman writes: "Bannon's quotation owes its force to the word 'platform'—in this usage, a scarce and valuable stage from which to broadcast. The platform's owner controls access and decides what gets play. To provide a platform is to share power, to convey legitimacy and to amplify voices. A movement's tactic is to gain access to platforms, and to use them to grow."

The currency on platforms is attention, and attention translates to revenue for the publishers. I have applied a three-part test in my attempts to answer the question "Should I platform this particular individual and their radical views?"

- Are the views expressed vile, radical, reprehensible, or otherwise undesirable from a societal standpoint? If the answer is no, then the interview is not one that needs to be analyzed in this way, and there is no issue with platforming the individual. If the answer is yes, I proceed to the second question.

- Are their views prevalent enough—or do they carry enough political capital in the discourse—that they warrant refutation lest they be allowed to fester and grow unchallenged? Again, if the answer is no, I opt out of doing the interview. If the answer is yes, I proceed to the third and final question.
- Am I able to be well-enough prepared to appropriately challenge and refute their views, or to give them "enough rope to hang themselves" if I were to conduct the interview?

The answers to any of these questions can change over time with regard to any particular individual or topic.

For example, in the immediate years before the 2015 Supreme Court decision *Obergefell v. Hodges*, which banned state-level bans on same-sex marriage, I would relatively frequently interview opponents of gay rights and homophobes of various stripes. Some would make religiously based arguments against same-sex marriage, others would have a so-called biological opposition, and some seemed merely confused and uninformed, falling into antigay bigotry as a result of culture and their environment rather than any well-thought-out opposition.

On the question of whether the views expressed were vile, radical, or reprehensible, the answer was absolutely yes.

On the question of whether the views were prevalent enough, or carried political capital in the discourse, the answer was absolutely yes. Same-sex marriage was not a right in all states at the time, homophobic ideologies were being used to raise massive amounts of money in opposition to gay rights, and it was very much an open question what the future of those rights would be. Lastly, at the time, as an ally of the LGBTQ+ movement, entrenched in the discourse and the debates, I felt confident I could substantively refute the arguments of these individuals.

Over time, the second question, of notability, shifted. After the 2015 SCOTUS decision, homophobia did not end, but the type of rabid overt homophobia opposing same-sex marriage dissipated. Groups like the Westboro Baptist Church no longer had even the mild cachet that they once had, and the debate over LGBTQ+ rights shifted to arguments over so-called religious freedom and employment discrimination. As a result, I've not conducted that type of interview since. This is not because the subject matter is no longer worthy, but because the totality of the answers to my three-question test no longer points in the direction of it being worthwhile to argue with retrograde radicals about same-sex marriage.

This brings us to the moral responsibility of making such platforming decisions. The absolute worst hypothetical outcome for such platforming decisions would be to convert more people to the radical views that the interviewer is actually attempting to oppose. There is also a consideration about the size of one's platform when making such decisions.

Every media outlet, be it a global news organization or a personal YouTube channel, wields varied levels of influence. The stories we tell, the guests we invite, and the topics we discuss shape perceptions, beliefs, and sometimes actions. Recognizing this immense power, there's a moral duty to use it judiciously. Merely stating that a platform is a "neutral space" or that it represents "free speech" does not absolve it of the consequences that stem from using it to feature certain individuals and topics. Even assuming that my three-question test has been passed, the responsibility that comes with free speech is to ensure that this freedom doesn't translate into tangible harm as a result of negligence or malice. There's a significant difference between promoting diverse voices and amplifying hate speech or disinformation. Responsible platforming requires discernment and a careful evaluation of whether the free speech of an extremist incites harm, perpetuates falsehoods, or destabilizes societal fabric.

The repercussions of platforming extremists aren't just confined to immediate reactions or public discourse; they linger, sometimes causing irreversible damage. The concept of "stochastic terrorism" is one that I have explored deeply on my program. At its core, stochastic terrorism refers to the use of mass communications to incite random actors to carry out violent acts. Given a large enough audience, repeatedly raising alarm about "dangerous Mexican immigrants" or "the evil Democrats," or whoever the scapegoat of the day is, it becomes increasingly likely that someone in the audience will actually take violent real-world action on the basis of what they are being told. There are sadly many such examples.

In 2009, Dr. George Tiller, one of the few physicians providing late-term abortions, was shot and killed by Scott Roeder.[4] Before his death, Dr. Tiller was demonized by anti-abortion groups and some media figures. Although no one directly ordered his assassination, the consistent vilification made such a violent act statistically more probable—the exact definition of stochastic terrorism.

In 2018, shooter Robert Bowers killed eleven worshippers at the Tree of Life synagogue in Pittsburgh, Pennsylvania.[5] Before the attack, he was known to post antisemitic content on social media platforms, where extremist views often get amplified. Bowers specifically believed in conspiracy theories suggesting Jews were aiding a migrant caravan heading toward the US, a narrative widely promoted among many right-wing media outlets.[6]

Without listing endless more examples like these, it should be mentioned that also part of this list is the Capitol insurrection, also known as the Trump riots, of January 6, 2021. The violent breach of the US Capitol by supporters of then president Donald Trump was the culmination of months of false claims about the 2020 presidential election being "stolen." While Trump never directly ordered the attack, his continued propagation of false information and inflammatory rhetoric set the stage for the event.

It's easy to brush off the influence of a single interview or debate, but when harmful ideologies find validation, even if unintentional, they take root deeper in society. Each of these incidents underscores the dangers of allowing extremist ideologies to be broadcast without challenge or context. They demonstrate the real-world consequences of rhetorical firestorms and the moral responsibility media entities and public figures bear in preventing stochastic terrorism.

Moral accountability means acknowledging this long-term impact and ensuring that platforming decisions prioritize the greater good over immediate gains or sensationalism.

The balance I've sought to strike when interviewing extremists involves a number of elements. First of all, the responsible interviewer will make absolutely clear that they do not agree with the views of the guest. This need not be done rudely or in a way that prevents a real conversation from taking place.

At the outset, it's crucial to establish a clear boundary between the interviewer and the extremist's viewpoint. While it's essential for an audience to know where the interviewer stands, it doesn't necessitate a confrontational or disrespectful tone. Instead, it's about firmly setting the stage and ensuring there's no ambiguity about the interviewer's stance. By clarifying my disagreement, I hope to safeguard against viewers mistaking my open platform as a silent endorsement.

Second, the interviewer must not only understand in advance the details of the views to be presented but be prepared to refute them, even if with a light touch, providing opportunities for the extremist to damage their own attempt to convince others. Before the interview, I immerse myself in understanding the intricacies of the extremist's viewpoint. This equips me to challenge any fallacies or inconsistencies in their stance, enabling a counternarrative to emerge during the dialogue. The aim isn't merely to react but to steer the conversation in a manner that highlights the flaws in their beliefs. It's not necessarily about being combative—although over the years, it has become combative many times—but about creating moments where the guest might inadvertently undermine their own ideology.

Often extremists come prepared with well-rehearsed talking points. An essential tactic is to redirect the conversation, forcing them to address points they might not have anticipated. This reframing can lead to unscripted responses, revealing the true depth (or lack thereof) of their understanding and beliefs.

Finally, the interviewer must not become emotionally compromised, which can be difficult to avoid. This is perhaps the most challenging aspect of my approach. The ideologies of many extremists can be deeply personal and offensive, especially when they target one's identity or community. It's a conscious effort not to let emotions take the wheel, especially when faced with deeply bigoted remarks.

As a Jewish interviewer, it takes effort not to react viscerally to the rantings of an antisemitic extremist. As an empathetic person, it takes nearly the same effort not to engage in a screaming match with a guest explaining that gay people deserve to be killed. This doesn't mean accepting or normalizing their beliefs, but rather not allowing those beliefs to derail the conversation's ultimate purpose: illumination and refutation.

It is essential to remember the broader aim of these interviews: responsible platforming. By engaging with extremists, the objective isn't to validate their perspective but to dissect it, understand its origins, and either present counterarguments directly or allow the extremist to expose the shortcomings of their beliefs. Ignoring these voices doesn't negate their existence; instead, it can inadvertently push them to more echo-chambered spaces, leading to further radicalization.

Another important consideration that is partially beyond our control is the reality that even well-prepared interviewers who do a good job of challenging these beliefs can end up having interviews clipped and re-published selectively, giving the false appearance that radical beliefs were welcomed by the interviewer. A ten-minute discussion where it is obvious that the interviewer rejects the radical beliefs of the guest can be cut into multiple thirty-second clips that might give the opposite opinion. At some level, this is difficult to predict and plan for, but it's a good idea to keep it in mind when conducting such interviews.

These are the components of responsible platforming, for which the net benefit far exceeds that of ignoring extremists, which rather than making them go away, can further radicalize them.

Where do we go from here on the issue of responsible platforming? As we experience a world where societal conversations are directed and shaped by digital interactions on the growing number of Internet-based platforms that disseminate information, the challenges of platforming grow more complex. Past encounters, including my own, teach lessons that serve as valuable guideposts to illuminate the risks yet remind us of the value of challenging bad ideas. However, sunlight as the best disinfectant is not always a perfect metaphor for these conversations. At the risk of taking the metaphor too far, sometimes sunlight causes weeds to grow. The digital landscape is ever evolving.

Past engagements with platforming underscore the myriad ways that these interactions can play out. While there have been instances where extremist beliefs gained traction in recent history, there have equally been moments where a well-conducted interview exposed the hollowness of radical ideologies. These interactions remind us of the power dynamics at play and the responsibility media entities bear. They emphasize the delicate balance between freedom of expression and the potential harm of unchecked amplification.

As we envision the road ahead, the guiding principles below come to mind.

Continued vigilance: The fluidity of the digital domain means that extremist ideologies can adapt and morph. Staying vigilant requires constant updates on the nuances of these ideologies, ensuring we're never caught offguard.

Education and training: Media outlets, podcasters, and content creators should invest in training that equips them with the skills to handle extremist viewpoints responsibly. This includes understanding rhetorical tactics employed by radicals and strategies to deconstruct them.

Collaboration: Media entities can benefit immensely from cross-collaboration, sharing insights and best practices. Collective action can foster a media environment less susceptible to the pitfalls of irresponsible platforming.

Self-reflection: Media entities must routinely evaluate their approach to platforming, assessing the impact of their content. Feedback from audiences and peers can offer valuable insights into areas of improvement. Some of the most valuable learning I've done after such interviews came from simply reviewing my own interviews a few days later, and sometimes again a few months later.

Promotion of constructive discourse: Encourage discussions that don't just spotlight extremist views but also highlight narratives that promote unity, understanding, and a shared sense of purpose. If the interviewer is not equipped to be the one challenging the views, inviting another guest who can assist may be a good idea.

Ultimately, the spread of extremist beliefs is not solely a function of the number of times the promulgators of those beliefs are interviewed. The spread depends on the quality and nature of those platforms. Well-informed and strategic interviews can do significant good by exposing and challenging radical beliefs, and it would go a long way toward pushing back against many of the issues discussed in earlier chapters. The correct approach is context-dependent and necessitates continuous reflection and adaptation to the media and cultural environment of the moment.

Platforming always comes with inherent risks, but with the correct tools, perspective, and intent, the risks can be dramatically mitigated, making the risk/reward calculation far more favorable to our side—the side of anti-extremists, anti-authoritarians, and those seeking informed engagement that turns a spotlight on extremism as something to be dissected, understood, and ultimately disarmed.

At times in the twentieth century, media was limited to a few trusted newspapers, radio shows, and, later, television broadcasts. The gatekeepers of these media sometimes but not always ensured a certain level of quality and reliability. However, the advent of the Internet and the democratization of content creation have blurred the lines between credible journalism and opinionated or even false content. This shift makes media literacy even more crucial today. Even with a basis in critical thinking and philosophy, those lacking the third competence of media literacy will struggle to effectively engage with the media world.

In the United States, the late twentieth century saw a burgeoning of media outlets with the advent of cable television and, subsequently, the Internet. Yet paradoxically, as access to information expanded, a solid foundation in media literacy did not grow proportionally. In fact, it arguably declined.

The emphasis in American education shifted toward standardized testing and rote memorization, often at the expense of subjects that fostered critical thinking, including media studies. This focus on test scores, sometimes to the detriment of broader educational goals, led to a generation less equipped to critically assess the vast array of media they encountered daily.

Deregulation in the 1980s played a significant role. The repeal of the Fairness Doctrine in 1987, which had required broadcasters to present contrasting views on controversial issues, gave way to more one-sided and opinionated programming. This further exacerbated divisions and made it harder for audiences to discern objective news from biased presentation.

Countries such as Finland, Sweden, and the Netherlands have long integrated media literacy into their core educational curricula. Finland, for instance, has been lauded for its comprehensive approach, teaching students to not just analyze media content but understand the economic and political interests that shape it. The results are evident: Finnish students consistently outperform their international counterparts in critical reading and media literacy assessments.[7]

Sweden's educational approach equips students to critically evaluate information, understand media structures, and even produce media. In the Netherlands, media literacy has been an officially strongly recommended subject since 2008, emphasizing both understanding and participation in media culture.[8]

At this point, media shapes public opinion and drives political discourse. Citizens who can critically assess the information presented are less susceptible to propaganda, false narratives, and sensationalism. They are better equipped to make informed decisions about their political beliefs and actions.

As is the case with most new technologies, particularly technologies for mass communication, there are pros and cons. The Internet age has given rise to numerous alternative and independent media outlets, allowing for a diversity of voices and viewpoints never before seen. It has also left media consumers exposed to unvetted and sometimes deliberately misleading information. Echo chambers—online spaces where one's beliefs are continuously reinforced by like-minded individuals—further exacerbate the problem.

The tangible impacts of the lack of media literacy are boundless, such as the spread of misinformation during recent election cycles. Fake news stories, propagated by foreign or domestic actors, found fertile ground among audiences unable to discern fact from fiction. A fake story claiming Pope Francis had endorsed Donald Trump was shared almost a million times.[9]

As with critical thinking, the lack of media literacy also regularly accelerates the spread of unfounded conspiracy theories. Without the skills to question and verify the authenticity of information sources, many fall prey to these baseless narratives.

In today's rapidly evolving media landscape, it is imperative to grasp the systemic forces that shape the news we consume. The process through which events transition from occurrences in the real world to stories on our screens or pages is intricate and fraught with bias. This selection is not random; it is influenced by a series of systemic factors that determine what is deemed newsworthy.

News agencies and media outlets operate within a competitive landscape, vying for the attention of audiences. This competition drives a preference for sensational stories—events that elicit strong emotions, usually shock, fear, or outrage. Consequently, negative events are disproportionately represented in the news, as they often have a greater sensational value. The majority of mainstream media outlets are for-profit entities, reliant on advertising revenue to sustain their operations. This financial dependency introduces an additional layer of bias in news selection and presentation, as stories that could alienate advertisers are often downplayed or omitted altogether.

The need for profitability also influences the kind of stories that are pursued in the first place. Media outlets are more likely to allocate resources to stories that promise higher viewer engagement, even if it comes at the expense of diversity and balance in reporting. The practicalities of news reporting also play a significant role in shaping media content. Media outlets are more likely to cover stories that are easily accessible to their reporters and camera crews. As a result, locations with a constant stream of newsworthy events, such as the White House, receive disproportionate coverage.

Understanding these systemic realities is the first step in becoming a critical and informed media consumer. It enables us to see beyond the surface of the news presented to us, prompting us to question why certain stories are told while others are not, and to seek out diverse and balanced sources of information.

Once the forces that drive the corporate media narrative are understood, we can move on to strategies for navigating corporate media. This requires a discerning eye and a balanced approach.

To navigate corporate media's bias, consumers must first recognize when a story is being sensationalized and question the motives behind its presentation. Second, balance can be sought by actively seeking out positive or neutral news to counterbalance the negative stories. Third, it is critical to conduct fact-checking by verifying information through multiple sources, especially for sensational stories.

The influence of advertisers should also be kept in mind. The reliance on advertising revenue means that corporate media outlets are beholden to the interests of their advertisers. This can lead to self-censorship, such as avoiding stories that could harm the interests of advertisers. It can also generate biased framing, where stories are presented in a way that aligns with advertisers' interests.

News consumers can combat this by identifying sponsorships and recognizing when sponsorships or partnerships could be influencing coverage. Also, seeking a diversity of reliable sources, including those with different funding models, can help to mitigate the impact of sponsor-related bias.

Understanding convenience bias is also important. Since stories that are easier and cheaper to cover receive more attention, we can counter this bias by seeking out underrepresented stories by proactively looking for news on topics or regions that typically receive less attention. Importantly, directly supporting independent media outlets, which are often more likely to cover stories that fall outside the convenience bias, is another tool.

By being aware of these biases and actively working to mitigate their effects, news consumers can maintain a healthier relationship with media, ensuring that their perspectives are informed, balanced, and resilient in the face of sensationalism and manipulation.

Also important is the realization that we do not need to be informed about the details of every media story right away. Corporate media's financial interests have worked to generate the idea that in order to be a "good" citizen, we must follow the news for its own sake, being aware of what is going on even when we can do little or nothing about it. In reality, this can generate anxiety and take up an inordinate amount of time that could be directed into other, healthier, more productive activities. The best way to prevent this is to decide in advance how much time we want to devote to following news, and through which media outlets. This is in contrast to simply getting drawn into endless news watching or social media scrolling with no clear objective or active decision about what we consume and why. With many news stories, including much so-called breaking news, we're better off informing ourselves at a slower pace, once the details have been reported accurately, rather than following minute-to-minute reporting that is often incomplete and ultimately corrected in the future.

By following this pyramid model, we can ensure that we are informed, critical, and resilient in the face of the challenges posed by the modern media landscape. As we integrate these practices into our daily lives, we become empowered to navigate the complexities of the news world, making informed decisions and contributing positively to our communities and society at large.

• • •

The last aspect of improving how we consume media is the mental health component. In an era of constant news updates and sensational headlines, maintaining mental well-being while staying informed can be a challenge.

First of all, it should be acknowledged that constant exposure to negative news can lead to stress, anxiety, and depression. One is not "weak" or "too sensitive" for coming to this realization, which is backed by significant research. One should learn to recognize signs of news fatigue, such as feeling overwhelmed, anxious, or apathetic toward current events.

Once identified, a set of strategies for taking breaks and maintaining balance can be established. For example, news consumers can allocate specific times of the day for news consumption and establish periods when they deliberately avoid news. In the bigger picture, consider periodic news detoxes, during which you disconnect from all news, to give your mind a break. This is not a "social media detox" or "technology detox," which often create the unrealistic expectation that one will be able to avoid technology. Rather, it's the specific replacement of news consumption with other subject matter to think about. That might be on devices, such as for movies or video games, and it might be nontechnological altogether, including outdoor activities, board games, exercise, or socializing. The idea is to test how one feels consuming less news, and then reapproach news in a proactive rather than passive way, consciously deciding the type of news we want to consume, as well as the schedule and frequency for consuming it.

It is always useful and beneficial to incorporate into your daily routine relaxation practices such as meditation and deep breathing exercises or hobbies that bring joy. It is also helpful to focus on what is within our control. The stoic philosophers, psychotherapists such as Viktor Frankl, and many others have written about this. Shifting our focus from global or national issues to local or personal actions where one can make a tangible impact can be incredibly useful. When following national or international news, making a direct impact may seem less likely. This is okay, as long as we're consuming a reasonable amount of this news. Sometimes one can make an impact on those issues, either through donations or through other means.

Don't hesitate to reach out to friends, family, or mental health professionals if you find the news is impacting your mental well-being. Many times, I hear from viewers that they simply have had to tune out of particularly tragic or sad stories, especially when they extend for weeks or months, including events such as wars or humanitarian crises. News can also be balanced with activities that promote positivity and well-being, such as spending time in nature, exercising, or volunteering.

Replacing or supplementing news with reading a wide variety of well-written books is one of the most effective techniques I have come across, along with going for a run or bike ride.

By implementing these strategies and learning from the experiences of others, you can create a balanced approach to news consumption that safeguards your mental health. The goal is not to disengage completely from current events but to find a sustainable way to stay informed while maintaining your well-being. Through conscious effort and intentional practices, you can foster a healthy relationship with news and media, ensuring that you remain a well-informed and resilient individual in today's fast-paced world.

CHAPTER 9

WHAT ELSE CAN WE DO?

N ow that we have a greater understanding of the Right's attack on critical thinking and some of the characteristics of a post-truth environment, how might we further effect meaningful change and go beyond
the often-repeated talking points about voting and engagement? Does
consuming political news, sending tweets, and participating in political
subreddits count as activism? Is calling your elected officials enough to be
considered "engaged" with the political system? Or is this merely political
hobbyism disguised as activism, accomplishing very little while consuming much of our time? And most importantly, which tactics and strategies
are actually effective at creating positive change in our communities?

Every new technology can bring with it unambiguously positive outcomes and opportunities while at the same time creating new problems.
The development of increasingly ubiquitous high-speed Internet, allowing for easy streaming of high-quality audio and video to desktop, laptop,
tablet, and mobile devices has been largely responsible for the growth
of independent political media. The explosive adoption of social media
platforms has without question allowed individuals to keep up with news,
politics, and current events around the world and in their communities.

Conversely, these same technologies have funneled endless hours of
people's time into watching videos, listening to podcasts, and sometimes
signing petitions, and it should be examined whether this constitutes productive political engagement and activism. The mildly pejorative term
"political hobbyism" has surfaced as a means of categorizing people who
follow politics, watch news, and maintain some basic level of awareness

of what is taking place around them in their immediate and more distant communities, without regard for whether this actually impacts those same communities.

Fundamentally, the consumption of media, along with the modest activities that often accompany it, such as talking to friends about politics and even signing petitions, do not have significant accomplishments to show for themselves. As a starting point, if increased political media consumption causes increased voting likelihood, it would start to make the case that political media consumption may be a valid precursor to basic political engagement, the act of voting. Unfortunately, the portion of news consumers who actually make calls to their elected officials, participate in local meetings to impact how their immediate municipality is being run, volunteer for campaigns, and engage in other ways is extremely limited.

It's important to talk about this issue not only as one of individual agency and personal responsibility but also within the context of the socioeconomic system that exists in the United States. Massive and powerful corporate forces would much prefer that the public merely consume political news and not actually engage with the political system. This preference is visible at every level. Social media companies make money from people spending more time on their platforms to further monetize that attention span. The more people watch political news on YouTube and share political articles on Facebook, the more money that parent companies Alphabet and Meta make, respectively. If the videos and articles were so inspiring and motivational that the users immediately left their televisions and computers and put their mobile phones away to go engage in real-world activism, social media companies would lose money.

But there's an even more notable systemic incentive to keep people as political hobbyists rather than true activists, and it has everything to do with the relationship of workers to employers. Tweeting during a break at work or watching a YouTube video from *The David Pakman Show* while on the subway after work is easy, and also nonthreatening to large corporations. It fits into the typical economic circumstances of an American adult. It also is unlikely to catalyze real systemic change.

The ways in which health care and housing are organized in the United States make activism more difficult. In addition, although we're focusing on activism beyond voting in this chapter, voting itself has become increasingly difficult in the United States as a result of voter suppression efforts by Republicans. Even beyond voter suppression, many other barriers remain.

Political hobbyism is the practice of consuming political news and participating in political discourse without actively engaging in substantive political actions that effect real-world change. Eitan Hersh, an associate professor of political science at Tufts University, writes extensively about political hobbyism in his book *Politics Is for Power*. During an interview he explained to me that political hobbyism is disproportionately hurting the political Left, stating that "on average, people whose preferences are more moderate, and actually more left, are the ones who are really succumbing to hobbyism the most."[1] This puts our attention on political hobbyism not only as a general problem to be considered but specifically as a mechanism that is hurting the Left, and as a result helping the political Right.

Political hobbyism is characterized by a passive engagement with politics, often mediated through online platforms or social media, where individuals observe, comment, and sometimes vociferously debate political events without ever transitioning into active participation or advocacy in the real world. The act becomes more about the consumption of politics as entertainment rather than a genuine effort to bring about change.

Historically, political discourse and action were closely intertwined. Before the age of instant information, civic engagement often meant active participation, such as attending town hall meetings, joining protests, or becoming members of political or advocacy groups. With the advent of the television age and later the Internet, the immediacy and convenience of obtaining news made it possible for individuals to participate in politics without ever leaving their homes. Over time, this passive consumption has become normalized, making the transition from observer to participant less common. Political hobbyism is not a new phenomenon per se, but the scale at which it's observed today, amplified by digital platforms, is unprecedented.

Social media platforms such as Facebook, YouTube, and X (formerly Twitter) have become the primary sources of news and political discourse for millions. The design of these platforms prioritizes engagement, and in many cases, this means the algorithms favor the most controversial or sensational content. As a result, users are often exposed to a skewed representation of political events, which can be more polarizing and less informative. The dopamine-driven feedback loops of likes, shares, and comments create an illusion of activism, when in reality they often only serve to reinforce existing beliefs without prompting real-world action. These platforms profit from users' prolonged engagement. The longer users stay, the more advertisements they see, generating revenue for the platform. This business model inadvertently discourages genuine political activism, as platforms have a vested interest in keeping users online rather than mobilizing them to act offline.

While staying informed is crucial, political hobbyism has its limits. Consuming vast amounts of political news without corresponding action can lead to feelings of cynicism, powerlessness, and burnout. It can create an echo chamber effect, where individuals only engage with like-minded individuals, further entrenching polarized views and reducing the possibility of meaningful discourse. This form of engagement lacks the collective power that has historically been necessary to effect significant political and societal change. Without transitioning from passive consumption to active engagement, the political landscape remains largely unaffected, irrespective of the number of retweets or likes a particular issue garners. This mode of engagement also often misses the nuance and depth of political issues. By focusing on headline-worthy events and sensational moments, the intricate and often less flashy work of policymaking, grassroots organizing, and advocacy gets overshadowed.

Understanding political hobbyism is vital for recognizing its limitations and the need to transition from passive consumption to active political engagement. Only through this shift can individuals and collectives harness the power to bring about the meaningful change they desire in their communities and the broader political landscape.

In the context of typical modern employment, the traditional nine-to-five job has extended its grasp, often consuming more hours than before with additional work-from-home expectations, constant email access, and more. This paradigm leaves individuals with less energy and time outside of work for active political participation. Moreover, the nature of work has shifted. The rise of the gig economy, with its unstable hours, lack of job security, and absence of standard benefits, has created an environment where workers are constantly in a mode of hustle. This instability results in civic engagement being pushed down the list of priorities.

Even aside from these more recent changes, many Americans are in a persistently precarious economic situation. According to the Federal Reserve's 2022 Economic Well-Being of US Households survey, 37 percent of Americans do not have the money to cover an unexpected $400 emergency expense without going into debt or using credit.[2]

The emotional and physical exhaustion of modern work culture, combined with the lack of job security, forms a formidable barrier to activism. It's no longer just about having the time—it's about having the mental bandwidth to engage in meaningful extracurricular activities after a grueling workday, and the financial circumstances to provide that.

There are also cultural and etiquette factors that prevent people from engaging in effective activism. In many large corporations, there exists an unspoken expectation to keep one's political views private, in order to prevent conflict or perceived bias. Many companies have policies discouraging or outright banning political discussions in the workplace, framing them as distractions. While the intention might be to maintain a harmonious work environment, the inadvertent effect is a suppression of political dialogue and engagement.

With the increasing digitization of our lives, employers' reach has extended beyond the office. Some companies monitor employees' social media activities, leading many individuals to self-censor out of fear of potential professional repercussions. When people's livelihoods might be at risk due to their political stances or activities, particularly when so many live paycheck to paycheck, it comes as no surprise that many opt for the path of least resistance: silence and nonengagement.

Not only is this a practical limitation at the individual level, but it can also impede the growth and development of activist movements. When individuals are hesitant to discuss societal issues due to potential backlash, it becomes increasingly difficult for movements to gain traction or for change to be instigated.

Regardless, work culture aside, for a vast segment of the American population, immediate economic concerns overshadow almost everything else. There are some specific additional realities in the American economy that make the type of activism discussed here more difficult. Beyond the general issues of limited disposable income, stagnant wages, no paid time off, and the sorts of limitations that make it hard to get time away from one's job to participate in activist actions are the particulars of the health-care system and housing costs.

The tethering of health care to employment, which is not done in many other countries, means that any form of dissent that jeopardizes employment can, in turn, jeopardize one's health coverage. In a country where medical bankruptcies are all too common, the stakes are immeasurably high. Since health insurance is linked to employment for most Americans, taking too much time off to go to rallies, or calling out of work as part of a mass action, could lead to loss of health insurance.

Additionally, the housing crisis, with its soaring rents and the increasing unaffordability of homes, further entrenches the economic insecurities faced by many. When individuals are burdened with the anxiety of making next month's rent or mortgage payment, their capacity to engage in extraneous political activities diminishes. Housing is so precarious and unaffordable for so many Americans that missing just a day or two of work can be the difference between affording rent or not. This friction is caused by the working conditions under so many employers in the United States and at the same time makes it less likely that workers will take the activist actions far more likely to result in political change. It is a system that perpetuates itself.

In addition, the overarching cloud of economic insecurity, amplified by debts from student loans and credit cards and the challenges of living paycheck to paycheck, further detracts from the populace's ability to actively engage in political activities. When daily survival becomes the primary concern, broader societal issues, no matter how pressing, are often sidelined.

Whether this is a deliberate situation fomented by the powers that be to prevent effective activism or merely a side effect of the US political climate today is irrelevant in the sense that its impact is identical. However, the Left is disproportionately affected by this status quo, which is another important aspect to consider.

The Left, historically renowned for its grassroots mobilization—from civil rights marches to antiwar protests—has seen a paradigm shift in recent decades. Direct action and feet on the ground have to a great degree been replaced by retweets, shares, and online petitions. The Right, however, has managed to retain a semblance of its grassroots essence, with movements like the Tea Party serving as testament. As progressive demographics embraced the convenience of the digital age, an inadvertent transition occurred, where offline activism diminished in the shadows of online virtue signaling.

Some left-leaning digital spaces have morphed into echo chambers, perpetuating similar sentiments without fostering diverse, actionable dialogue. Hashtags trend and virtual rallies gain traction, but when it's time to vote, rally, or protest in the real world, the numbers are anemic. In contrast, right-wing digital campaigns often spill onto the streets. An example that stands out is the Right's campaign against certain reproductive rights. Vocal online opposition from the Left was frequently overshadowed by the Right's offline mobilization, culminating in legislative shifts, in great part thanks to the chain of events set off by Donald Trump's election, and then the Supreme Court justices nominated by Trump.

Online engagement doesn't always translate into policy impact. The Left's advocacy for climate change solutions and action, for instance, dominates the digital realm. Yet substantive policy debates in legislative chambers often lack the same fervor. Despite overwhelming online support, unfortunate realities such as lobbying, corporate interests, and a lack of coordinated grassroots efforts halt progress. On the other hand, the Right, despite facing online criticism, has pushed deregulatory agendas, capitalizing on the Left's offline inertia.

The Left's shift from grassroots to online communities has diluted its real-world impact. While digital activism reaches a wider audience, its transient nature makes sustained impact challenging. The Right's persistence with traditional mobilization offers them tangible advantages. Take the case of unionized efforts: while the Left celebrates labor rights online, right-wing efforts in some states have weakened union powers, with real consequences for workers' rights.

Consider the 2016 US presidential election. Bernie Sanders's campaign saw unprecedented online support, especially among young progressives. Yet, when it came to primary results, the surge didn't fully materialize. Conversely, Donald Trump's right-wing base, although active online, showcased impressive on-the-ground mobilization, ultimately securing him the presidency.

Even more notably, the online support for Bernie Sanders during the Democratic presidential primary in 2020 left some progressives shocked at the degree to which Joe Biden overwhelmed the other candidates once primary voting actually started. Another instance is gun control. Despite mass online campaigns by the Left after mass shootings, right-wing offline lobbying often thwarts legislative changes. The Left's disengagement not only costs them elections but also results in long-term policy setbacks, making the urgency for balanced engagement palpable.

The Left's dissonance between online advocacy and offline action has real-world ramifications. While the digital realm amplifies voices, tangible change mandates feet on the ground, coordinated efforts, and sustained engagement. A big-picture rethink may be necessary.

As covered earlier in the book, the right to vote, despite being a fundamental democratic principle, has been perpetually embroiled in American sociopolitical discourse. Nevertheless, the act of voting is still impeded by obstacles that predominantly affect marginalized and economically disadvantaged populations.

But how can activists go beyond voting, signing petitions, and calling elected officials if they so choose and are able to do so logistically? This is not a list of forms of activism that I necessarily recommend people act on in all or some cases, but the sorts of activities that can more quickly have an impact, even though they often aren't possible because of economic and practical realities, as well as familial and legal considerations.

MASS RALLIES

Mass rallies in urban centers and state capitals represent a poignant visual and symbolic embodiment of collective dissatisfaction and demand for change. A sea of individuals unified by a common cause, from the Civil Rights Movement to climate change protests, showcases solidarity, disrupts everyday operations, and often necessitates a response from political leadership.

Historically, these events have been powerful platforms for voicing collective dissent and catalyzing change. The March on Washington, DC, in 1963 where Martin Luther King Jr. delivered his iconic "I Have a Dream" speech is near the top of the list. Antinuclear protests in New York's Central Park in 1982 were ultimately one of the largest political protest efforts in the US up to that point, propelling the antinuclear movement into the national and international spotlight. The Tahrir Square protests in Egypt in 2011 in opposition to President Hosni Mubarak's regime utilized social media extensively and initiated a chain of events that ultimately altered the political landscape of the Middle East.

STRATEGIC MASS ABSENCES FROM WORK

Strategic work stoppages or boycotts exert pressure by disrupting economic activities. General strikes and boycott days can diminish corporate profits and governmental tax revenues, thus compelling a reconsideration of policies or practices that are being protested against.

Such actions have proven to be potent tools in advocating for workers' rights and eliciting substantial change. The 1936–37 Flint Sit-Down Strike in Michigan is a notable example: employees, unsatisfied with their working conditions and remuneration, occupied factories and halted production, compelling General Motors to recognize the United Automobile Workers union. Another notable instance occurred in 1980 in Poland, where the Solidarity movement, led by Lech Wałęsa, organized widespread strikes across the nation's shipyards and factories, challenging the communist government and ultimately paving the way for democratic reform in Poland. These instances elucidate how strategic work stoppages can disrupt economic activity and force attention toward the grievances and demands of the working class, sparking legislative and systemic changes that reverberate through time.

COORDINATED DEBT DEFAULTS

Facilitating mass nonpayment of debts, or boycotting certain financial products and institutions, can potentially destabilize economic structures, forcing financial entities to negotiate or reconsider their practices. This was somewhat mirrored in moments of the Occupy Wall Street movement, highlighting the potentials of collective economic resistance.

Similar to strategic work absences, coordinated debt defaults focus on disrupting economic systems. During the Argentine economic crisis in 2001–2, various civil society groups encouraged citizens to withdraw their money from banks, default on debts, and participate in mass protests to voice their dissatisfaction with their government's and the International Monetary Fund's policies, pushing the nation in a different economic direction.

Another example would be the "Can't Pay, Won't Pay" campaign in the United Kingdom during the 1980s. This was essentially a debt resistance strategy against the Thatcher government's imposition of the Community Charge (or "Poll Tax"), which was seen as unfairly burdening the poor. Large-scale nonpayment campaigns, involving millions of citizens refusing to pay the tax, significantly impacted government revenues and became a massive administrative burden, ultimately playing a role in both the policy's repeal and Margaret Thatcher's resignation as prime minister.

CIVIL DISOBEDIENCE

Civil disobedience, like noncooperation with specific laws or enacting blockades, can serve as a powerful political tool. For instance, the Civil Rights Movement effectively utilized noncooperation and civil resistance to challenge and change racially unjust laws and practices.

Civil disobedience has a rich history as a form of nonviolent protest, wherein participants deliberately break certain laws to highlight injustice and prompt change. The civil rights era provides multiple examples of civil disobedience. Perhaps most notable among them is the Montgomery bus boycott of 1955–56, in which African Americans, led by figures such as Mrs. Rosa Parks and Dr. Martin Luther King Jr., refused to comply with segregated bus systems. Their nonviolent refusal to adhere to unjust laws significantly impacted the bus system and garnered wide-reaching attention, marking a crucial point in the battle against segregation and racial injustice in the US.

One of the most famed examples is Mahatma Gandhi's salt march in 1930. In protest against the oppressive salt taxes imposed by the British colonial rulers in India, Gandhi led thousands on a 240-mile march to the Arabian Sea to make their own salt.

COMMUNITY ORGANIZING FOR LOCAL CHANGE

Although it is often more appealing to get involved in national politics, changes can sometimes be effected more quickly at the local level.

Engaging in community organizing, through establishing local councils or developing community resources, enables autonomy and resilience. Creating and supporting local initiatives such as food co-ops or community health care can establish alternative, sustainable structures.

The Chicago Freedom Movement of the 1960s is a quintessential example; Martin Luther King Jr. and the Southern Christian Leadership Conference worked with local organizations in Chicago to address racial segregation and economic inequalities in the city. This movement utilized a community organizing approach, engaging local residents in protests, marches, and rallies, but also creating community-run institutions and initiatives aimed at directly addressing local needs and issues.

In a different era and context, Harvey Milk, the first openly gay elected official in California, organized communities in San Francisco in the 1970s to fight discrimination against the LGBTQ+ community. He cultivated solidarity among disparate groups, mobilizing a grassroots movement that eventually led to the passing of a gay rights ordinance in the city, offering new antidiscrimination protections for gay and lesbian individuals.

ECONOMIC INTERVENTIONS

Promoting and nurturing alternative economic systems, such as local currencies or mass divestment from certain industries, can pivot financial power and influence away from oppressive economic structures.

An excellent example is the anti-apartheid movement in South Africa, which spanned several decades and sought to end apartheid policies. Activists worldwide engaged in diverse economic interventions, such as advocating for divestments from companies involved with the South African regime. In the 1980s, the call for disinvestment from South Africa was heeded by numerous entities, including universities and corporations, applying substantial economic and political pressure that contributed to dismantling apartheid policies.

The grape boycott led by Cesar Chavez and Dolores Huerta in the 1960s and 1970s in the United States aimed at improving the working conditions of farm laborers. By urging consumers not to buy grapes, they sought to economically pressure growers to provide better wages and conditions for workers, achieving significant successes in terms of labor rights and contracts.

CULTIVATING SOCIAL AND CULTURAL MOVEMENTS

Utilizing cultural jamming or leveraging arts and performative pro-tests can provide powerful, subversive commentaries on prevailing social issues, utilizing culture as a medium of resistance and critique. These are usually broader movements that can encompass, at the tactical level, many of the other techniques discussed in this section.

The Civil Rights Movement of the 1950s and 1960s, the movement for women's suffrage in the late nineteenth and early twentieth centuries, and the LGBTQ+ rights movement dating back to the late 1960s and early 1970s are all examples of bigger-picture sociocultural movements. The #MeToo movement, which initiated a global discussion around sexual harassment and assault, is another example.

DIRECT ACTIONS

Engaging in direct actions such as sit-ins or physically dismantling oppressive structures can halt or disrupt activities and symbolically con-test unjust systems, as witnessed historically in the Greensboro and Nash-ville sit-ins of 1960.

Many of these direct actions took place within the context of broader movements mentioned in this section. During the salt march in 1930s India, protesters used the tactic of nonviolent civil disobedience through the direct production of salt. During the Civil Rights Movement, sit-ins were utilized extensively as a tool to highlight the absurdity and cruelty of segregation policies. During the Occupy Wall Street movement in 2011, activists occupied Zuccotti Park in New York City's financial district. In-digenous peoples, particularly the Standing Rock Sioux, and their allies engaged in direct action by establishing resistance camps and physically obstructing construction sites to halt the progress of the Dakota Access Pipeline in 2016 and 2017.

The women's suffrage movement famously held a march in Wash-ington, DC, organized by Alice Paul, prior to the inauguration of Pres-ident Woodrow Wilson in 1913. They marched from the Capitol, down Pennsylvania Avenue, ending at the Treasury Building. The violence and harassment faced by the marchers garnered widespread media coverage, leading the Senate to hold an inquiry into the poor police protection provided during the parade. The resulting investigation embarrassed the authorities and highlighted the determination and seriousness of the suffrage movement. Following the parade, Alice Paul and her colleagues formed the Congressional Union for Woman Suffrage, which later became the National Woman's Party (NWP). The heightened visibility and intensified pressure from suffrage activists contributed to the eventual passage of the Nineteenth Amendment to the US Constitution.

GUERRILLA COMMUNICATION

Guerrilla communication, through subvertising—the process of subverting advertisements to spoof, parody, satirize, and flip the meaning of messages found in commercial advertising—and flash mobs, presents unexpected, often subversive narratives in public spaces, challenging mainstream discourses and introducing alternative perspectives in accessible and often impactful ways.

Some examples include the Barbie Liberation Organization, which in the 1990s swapped the voice boxes of Barbie dolls and GI Joe action figures and returned them to stores to highlight the ways in which the toys themselves perpetuated gender stereotypes. The Yes Men target and mock large corporations and government entities, for example, by setting up fake websites appearing to represent entities such as the World Trade Organization or Dow Chemical, and using those platforms to release false press statements or create parody products.

Artists have used projections on the sides of well-known buildings to communicate messages. In 2018, an artist and activist projected the word "Sh*thole" along with poop emojis onto the Trump International Hotel in Washington, DC, co-opting the president's controversial descriptor of certain countries and redirecting it in a critical manner.

These guerrilla communication tactics, utilizing surprise, humor, or unanticipated interventions in public or media spaces, aim to disrupt normalcy and provoke thought, drawing attention to specific issues or messages in unconventional ways.

HARNESSING ALTERNATIVE AND INDEPENDENT MEDIA

Fostering alternative media by supporting independent journalism or creating new platforms amplifies voices that are often marginalized in mainstream narratives, thereby constructing channels for more diverse and authentic stories. This is the primary form of activism I have chosen to engage in, and it has been by far the most effective for me as an individual and through my audience.

The proliferation of podcasts and independent online news platforms provides a diverse array of voices and perspectives on political and social issues. Much of this owes a debt to the development of the very technologies that also bring their own concerns and create new problems. Even before these more recent technological innovations, pirate radio and citizen journalism already filled this role to some degree. By creating or tapping into these alternative and independent media platforms, activists and social movements can articulate their narratives and perspectives on their own terms, reaching global audiences and mobilizing support without relying on traditional media outlets. This allows for a more unfiltered and direct communication strategy with the public and can help coordinate and amplify activist efforts.

LEVERAGING LEGAL ACTION

Engaging in public interest litigation or providing legal support for activists can challenge and reshape policy from within the justice system, offering a simultaneous attack against oppressive structures within their own legal frameworks.

Although often more expensive and requiring more coordination and resources, legal action can sometimes lead to some of the most significant changes. The landmark *Brown v. Board of Education* Supreme Court case from 1954, which declared state laws establishing racially segregated schools to be unconstitutional, was the culmination of significant activism involving numerous organizations. Legal actions against big tobacco in the late 1990s led to massive settlements and increased regulations. Many other such examples could be considered.

All of these strategies must be carefully evaluated and judiciously utilized. Sometimes there can be legal risk to some of them, depending on the prevailing laws where they are being used. The point is not to encourage lawbreaking—most utilizations of these strategies are completely legal—but to consider that a blend of these approaches, tailored to specific contexts and causes, can encourage a broader culture of effective activism and help build a robust ecosystem for meeting challenges and solving real problems.

History teaches us that gradual change, not accelerationism, has led to the most sustained progressive achievements over time.

Accelerationists believe that to achieve progress, pushing to the extreme is necessary. Often, deliberately collapsing a subpar or broken system is necessary in order to make way for something new. Simply speaking, "Tear it down to build it back up" encompasses the general approach of accelerationism. Accelerationists often end up opposing positive changes on the basis that they are not significant enough, and they may further entrench the system we have by making it only slightly better, thus reducing the incentive to replace the system completely.

This is not the approach that I adhere to. Instead, I am an incrementalist. Incrementalists believe in making continuous, sometimes gradual, step-by-step changes with the belief that over time, the sum total of these gradual changes will significantly improve society. History and common sense are on the side of incrementalists. Accelerationists often ignore the reality that the chaos of an accelerationist approach, if it were to succeed in the total destruction of a system, would ultimately be counterproductive and could delay progress even further. Accelerationism can destroy the parts of a system that are working along with the ones that are not. Accelerationism, once successful in tearing down the existing system, can end up with parties in power in the new system that are just as bad as or even worse than those in the system that was taken down. In short, accelerationism can cause unpredictable changes, often creating as many new problems as it may solve.

At a societal level, the degree of upheaval that would be required for the accelerationist approach to reach its ultimate goal would be so chaotic and disorganized that it would be an impediment to people's ability to live safe and normal lives, and could negatively impact an entire generation of young people irreversibly.

Most importantly, the historical evidence for accelerationism's successes is slim, while the evidence for the success of incrementalism, particularly in the United States, is overwhelming.

The progressive Left in the United States is correct to feel that not enough is getting done, and that despite decades of activism, many of the same problems remain unsolved. This often leads to the growing sense of futility about being involved in politics that earlier chapters have explored. However, this perspective is dangerous in a number of ways. It happens to be exactly what the American right wing wants the Left to feel so that they will abandon their activism, allowing the Right even more unobstructed radicalization. It is also factually inaccurate to believe that not much progress has been made.

Even when change happens quickly in a historical context, such as over ten to fifteen years, it takes place too slowly for major changes to feel fast at the pace of daily life. This is visible in technology. Applied to politics, it often feels as though certain fights have been taking place nearly forever, or for as long as people care to remember. Progressive battles over universal health care, climate change, income equality, net neutrality, and race relations have been ubiquitous for decades, even centuries, and while these battles are still being fought, an objective analysis shows that, step-by-step, incrementally, dramatic improvements have been made.

On health care, for example, the last fifteen years have seen incredible progress. In terms of access, Obamacare codified important requirements on insurers, including protections for those with preexisting conditions, the ability of children to stay on parents' insurance until age twenty-six, and many others. More than forty-one states plus Washington, DC, now run their own state Medicaid equivalent programs, providing health insurance to those lacking the ability to pay. President Joe Biden continued by expanding access to Medicaid and getting pharmaceutical companies to negotiate lower prices to Medicare for ten of the most commonly used medications, a major achievement still in progress as of this writing.

Ted Kennedy, the late Democratic senator from Massachusetts, was a major advocate of this incrementalist approach, and his legacy of successes is the best testament to the strategy's effectiveness. As explored by Harvard business professor Rosabeth Moss Kanter in 2009, "Even when Kennedy could not move the needle forward on really big change, he supported incremental improvements (children's health insurance), which meant that he survived in office long enough for his big agenda to come close to being enacted."[3]

Kanter may appear to be approaching this from a strictly pragmatic perspective of what would be useful to Kennedy in winning his next election, but her analysis accurately considers that at the end of a political term, all voters should be asking, "What has been accomplished?" This is a fair question not only from a standpoint of voting but also progress, and for better or worse, supporting revolutionary change but accomplishing nothing isn't merely a failure of optics—it's an actual failure to do anything that would improve the lives of one's constituents.

A real-world example of this was visible in the "no" votes on President Joe Biden's infrastructure bill in late 2021. Democratic members of Congress Alexandria Ocasio-Cortez, Ilhan Omar, Rashida Tlaib, Jamaal Bowman, Cori Bush, and Ayanna Pressley opposed their own party's bill, not because it went too far but because it did not go far enough. This is a perfect example of rejecting a small step because it wasn't a big enough step, but also of the counterproductive consequence of pushing more voters to the middle rather than the left by publicly opposing a bill that was overwhelmingly liked by Democratic voters.

Just as important as recognizing the progress is accepting that these problems have not been solved. The point is not to suggest complacency but to energize ourselves for further change by recognizing the successes that have taken place in the past. Three of the major periods of progressive achievement in the United States were the Progressive Era, the New Deal era, and the civil rights era.

THE PROGRESSIVE ERA (1890S TO 1920S)

The Progressive Era saw numerous monumental achievements built on an even larger number of incremental advancements, all layered onto decades of slow progress. Antitrust legislation such as the Sherman Anti-Trust Act of 1890 and the Clayton Antitrust Act of 1914 established a framework for curbing monopoly power and fostering competition. The Seventeenth Amendment, ratified in 1913, allowed senators to be elected directly instead of being chosen by state legislatures. The Pure Food and Drug Act of 1906 required that food and drugs be labeled accurately and established the FDA to oversee these regulations. The Federal Reserve was established in 1913. In 1920, the Nineteenth Amendment to the Constitution was ratified, granting women the right to vote.

All of these achievements were influenced by and built on earlier muckraking journalism that shed light on corporate malpractice, political corruption, and societal problems. The activist movements that originated

and grew in the 1890s laid the groundwork for many Progressive Era reforms, especially regarding big business and government accountability.

In the case of the Nineteenth Amendment, smaller, local suffrage victories began as early as the 1860s in western territories such as Wyoming,
which seemed comparatively small at the time. Grassroots movements
and local-level progressive reforms of all kinds were precursors to national changes.

Many of these eventual victories were also based on specific judicial
appointments to the Supreme Court. For example, President Theodore
Roosevelt, who served from 1901 to 1909, appointed Oliver Wendell
Holmes Jr. to the Supreme Court. Holmes became an influential progressive voice on the court and was a major factor in many of these eventual
victories. Analogizing to the 2016 election, the victory of Donald Trump
over Hillary Clinton was not immediately relevant in terms of Supreme
Court decisions, but through the eventual nominations made by Trump,
Roe v. Wade was ultimately overturned. The selection of Holmes by Roosevelt is another reminder of the potential impact of presidential elections
on future law through the Supreme Court.

Each of these changes and steps forward might have seemed small
on their own, much like accelerationists today would decry many more
recent achievements as merely small steps, but together they drastically
changed the face of American governance and industry, setting up foundations that lead to further change throughout the twentieth century.

THE NEW DEAL ERA (1930S)

Progressive achievements during the New Deal era were absolutely massive. The Social Security Act of 1935 created the Social Security program
to provide financial support for the elderly, disabled, and unemployed,
now one of the hallmarks of the American safety net. The Securities Ex-
change Act of 1934 founded the SEC and regulated the stock market to
prevent the sort of speculative bubbles that led to the Great Depression.
In 1935, the National Labor Relations Act gave workers the right to form
unions and collectively bargain. The Wagner Act, which bolstered labor
rights further, leading to a massive increase in labor union membership,
was also passed in 1935. Through the New Deal, key agencies and programs were created, including the Civilian Conservation Corps (CCC),

Public Works Administration (PWA), and the Works Progress Administration (WPA).

Launched in 1933, the CCC was designed to provide jobs for young men and relieve families who had difficulty finding jobs during the Great Depression. It employed over 2.5 million young men who built trails, lodges, and related facilities in more than eight hundred parks nationwide. It also initiated projects to combat soil erosion and maintain forest lands, planted billions of trees to reforest America, and developed state parks and created infrastructure that is still in use today.

The PWA was a large-scale public works construction agency intended to stimulate the economy and provide jobs. It funded the construction of more than thirty-four thousand projects, including airports, electricity-generating dams, aircraft carriers, schools, and hospitals, including the Grand Coulee Dam, the Triborough Bridge, and the Lincoln Tunnel.

Lastly, the WPA was designed to create jobs for the unemployed by building public buildings and roads and executing various arts projects. It employed roughly 8.5 million people over its existence, constructed or repaired about 650,000 miles of roads, 125,000 public buildings, and 8,000 parks, and left an enduring legacy in infrastructure, culture, and arts.

All of the major progress during this critical era under President Franklin D. Roosevelt was on the shoulders of the incremental change that started during the 1920s and was built on earlier incremental steps. Prior to the massive New Deal legislative push, smaller programs and agencies were set up as a trial to gauge their effectiveness. The First New Deal of 1933 was a precursor to the more extensive legislation that would come in 1935 and later, and it included banking reforms like the Emergency Banking Act and the Glass-Steagall Act, agricultural reforms, industrial reforms, and other job creation programs.

The early efforts of labor organizers in the 1920s set the stage for labor-related New Deal policies. The financial panics in the 150 years leading to the Great Depression exposed the need for regulatory measures, which were built on existing, albeit limited, financial regulations. Grassroots movements and local relief programs served as models for federal New Deal programs.

Much of the progress also depended on the Supreme Court shaped by FDR. Initially he faced a Supreme Court that struck down key New

Deal legislation. His attempt to "pack the court" in 1937 was unsuccessful. However, through natural turnover he was able to appoint eight justices to the Supreme Court. Those appointments ensured a more favorable judicial climate for his policies.

Each New Deal policy, while focused on immediate relief, also put in place long-term structural changes to the US economy and government's role in society.

THE CIVIL RIGHTS ERA (1950S AND 1960S)

In the first chapter, the story of the breakage of American politics starts with the civil rights era. The reason why this era started so much of the downhill spiral of the American right wing was indeed because it was such a successful era for achieving progressive change. The Civil Rights Act of 1964 outlawed discrimination based on race, color, religion, sex, or national origin. The Voting Rights Act of 1965 outlawed racial discrimination in voting, specifically targeting barriers to Black enfranchisement in the South. The 1954 Supreme Court decision *Brown v. Board of Education* declared racial segregation in public schools unconstitutional.

Once again, these major achievements depended on earlier incremental steps. The NAACP's legal battles in the early twentieth century laid the groundwork for larger court victories like *Brown*. The grassroots activism of the 1950s, such as the Montgomery bus boycott, built momentum for national legislative change. Each legal and legislative victory was built on earlier actions, such as Truman's integration of the military in 1948.

Brown v. Board of Education built on earlier cases like *Missouri ex rel. Gaines v. Canada* (1938) and *Sweatt v. Painter* (1950), which chipped away at the "separate but equal" doctrine. Before the national legislation, grassroots movements and smaller local or state rulings challenged and made dents in segregationist policies. The Montgomery bus boycott in 1955 and the desegregation of Little Rock Central High School in 1957 served as precursors to larger legislative changes.

Once again, judicial appointments played an important role. Dwight D. Eisenhower, president from 1953 to 1961, appointed Earl Warren as chief justice in 1953. The Warren court became known for its progressive rulings, especially in the area of civil rights. Eisenhower also appointed

William J. Brennan Jr., another key liberal voice. Their contributions were instrumental in many of the civil rights rulings of the era.

The cumulative effect of these victories led to the dismantling of legal Jim Crow in the South and laid the foundation for ongoing civil rights movements, from women's rights to LGBTQ+ rights.

In each of these three eras, while individual achievements were incremental, the aggregate changes they brought were transformative for American society. By illustrating the foundational steps leading up to these pivotal moments, it becomes evident that monumental societal shifts often arise as a culmination of smaller, incremental changes. Each legislative achievement, court decision, or policy change is a building block, and each election can have far-reaching consequences on the course of history. All three of these major eras of progress would have seemed relatively small and slow-moving at the time, much like the leftward changes of the 1990s, 2000s, and beyond, but cumulatively, they represent extraordinary change and progress.

Beyond legislation, the incrementalist versus accelerationist conversation can and must also be applied to elections themselves. This includes decisions regarding primaries, state versus national strategy, and other critical areas of democracy.

It is vital to understand that the US electoral system has historically lent itself to gradual change rather than sharp, seismic shifts. At its core, incrementalism is about achieving small but steady policy and electoral victories, each building on the last, and many of the checks and balances that make up the American system are part of the environment that foments this incrementalism. Whether one is for or against this, it is the reality and must inform the Left's approach on this issue. It can be analogized to a game of chess where each move is calculated, deliberate, and anticipatory of the next series of plays. Although sometimes "traps" can be used in the first few moves to quickly win a game against a distracted or inexperienced opponent, those traps quickly stop working in most chess situations, and thus a calculated longer-term strategy is necessary. The value of such a methodology lies not just in the immediacy of the gains but also in laying a foundation for future successes.

Political incumbency also carries significant weight. Once in office, an official has access to resources, established networks, and, crucially, name recognition. An established record can also be a powerful tool, allowing incumbents to showcase their achievements. Conversely, challenging an incumbent comes with its risks, such as potentially splitting the vote, creating intraparty divisions, and risking the ire of established party figures. Thus, before seeking to unseat an incumbent, there's a need to weigh the costs and benefits carefully. Sometimes these reality checks can generate a reaction from accelerationists that one is conceding to the establishment or giving up on leftward progress by merely considering these facts, but this is misguided. The risk is that when these realities are ignored, even more damage can be done than simply doing nothing at all, which is even more regrettable.

An accelerationist view, applied to elections, often prefers to challenge and primary existing Democratic elected officials on the basis that they are "not progressive enough." For example, in the early twenty-first century, this conversation often revolved around primary challenges to West Virginia senator Joe Manchin, a Democrat who was on the more moderate side of the party. Accelerationists wanted to primary him, while incrementalists rightly recognized that a more progressive Democrat would likely lose in conservative West Virginia, and that resources and effort would be better invested in attempting to flip other seats currently held by Republicans to Democrats.

History is rife with examples of primary challenges—some successful, some not. The dynamics of a primary challenge are unique. The balance between ideological purity and broader electoral strategy plays out in real time. Successful primary challenges often revolve around an incumbent's misalignment with their constituency or broader public sentiment. Yet challenges that simply stem from an ideological rift, without a broader strategy in place, can lead to electoral defeats in general elections.

Incrementalism in electoral politics often thrives on coalition building. Coalitions offer a chance to pool resources, share voter bases, and reach constituencies that might otherwise be out of reach. Historically, broad coalitions have been the bedrock of significant legislative victories. It's not just about forming alliances within the party but reaching across the aisle and working with moderate factions of the opposition, focusing on shared objectives rather than divisive issues.

Elections are as much about *where* you compete as they are about *how* you compete. Focusing on flippable districts or seats offers a chance to make meaningful gains with limited resources. This doesn't mean ignoring staunchly partisan areas but rather prioritizing battles that can be won. State legislatures also play a pivotal role in shaping the broader political landscape, especially when it comes to redistricting. An incremental approach acknowledges the importance of these smaller yet significant battlegrounds.

Another aspect to this is time horizon. An incremental approach is inherently long-term. It's about planting seeds today that will grow in future electoral cycles. This involves cultivating future leaders, investing in activist infrastructure, and initiating voter registration and education drives. By nurturing grassroots movements, the party can ensure a steady stream of leaders and activists ready to carry the mantle forward. A strong bullpen of future leaders and activists also allows flexibility in terms of location and timing for well-thought-out primaries and challenges, rather than feeling forced into shortsighted decisions due to a lack of options in the future.

Compromise is often seen as a dirty word in politics, but in the world of incrementalism, it's a tactical tool. It's about recognizing that sometimes, partial victories can pave the way for more significant gains down the line. History is filled with examples where initial compromises have led to larger, more profound policy achievements in subsequent years. It's important not to misunderstand the context of compromise. Compromising with political extremists, who in many cases have utterly deplorable and radical views, is not what is at issue here. In fact, compromise with such people is often impossible, regardless of the Left's intentions. Instead, this is about being as practical and realistic as possible in assessing when there is a gain to be had, and in working to secure that gain.

Politics, at its core, is a marathon, not a sprint. Using a different analogy, it's important to know that the war is not won or lost in one battle. If one prefers, a journey of a thousand miles starts with the first step. The allure of rapid change is undeniably potent, and can even work to encourage new activists to enter the political world. However, the arc of history bends toward perseverance, and toward making small yet consistent gains. The resilience and adaptability of an incremental approach stand as a testament to its enduring power in the dynamic landscape of American politics.

· · ·

Incrementalism is not without its legitimate criticisms, and they are worth considering here. Every one of these criticisms has valid elements and raises warranted concerns, but at the same time does not contradict the historical and practical realities that make incrementalism the better approach.

PACE OF CHANGE

Near the top of the list of criticisms of incrementalism is that of the perceived slow pace of change that comes with its adoption. Detractors argue that there are pressing issues, like climate change or social justice, that require immediate and radical solutions, not gradual measures.

However, while the pace can be slow, incrementalism is pragmatic. History has shown that sudden, sweeping changes often face stronger resistance and backlash, whereas small, strategic steps can be more durable, gaining wider acceptance over time. They also can be considered from a legal perspective more carefully, ideally avoiding their being ultimately overturned or reversed through legal means. Moreover, what seems slow in the short term can lead to transformative change in the long run.

EMPOWERING THE OPPOSITION

Critics of incrementalism argue that by being willing to compromise and make small concessions, incrementalism might inadvertently empower and embolden radical opposition, allowing them to hijack the narrative. In addition, if the Left adopts incrementalism, but the Right does not, the Right can much more quickly make progress on their agenda when they find themselves in power, rapidly outdoing the impact of the Left's incrementalist approach.

In reality, the outcomes are often the opposite. While incrementalism can be seen as a sign of weakness, it also functions as a strategic tool to isolate extremist views and build broader coalitions. Furthermore, refusing to compromise can lead to political stalemate, preventing any progress whatsoever.

PERPETUATING INJUSTICE

Accelerationists often argue that the small reforms of incrementalism ignore the urgent and emergency status of our system, leaving critical, fundamental problems unaddressed, thereby perpetuating injustices. In other words, the idea is that small changes to radically unjust systems still leave them radically unjust.

In reality, incrementalism doesn't imply any satisfaction or tolerance whatsoever with minimal reforms. Instead, it suggests a phased approach to addressing systemic issues. Problems aren't being ignored; they are simply being addressed in stages. These smaller steps can pave the way for more significant reforms in the future and are often more feasible in the present political climate. In many cases, the larger reforms come more easily after a period of incremental change has moved the status quo closer to the ultimate end point, and can end up generating less resistance as the eventual goal is approached.

RISK OF COMPLACENCY

Achieving a number of small victories could feel like real change has been accomplished, when in reality it is a false feeling of momentum. As the critics state it, celebrating minor victories could lead to complacency and a loss of momentum for more substantial changes.

In truth, small victories not only build momentum but encourage activists to continue creating change; they also add up over time, often more quickly than might be obvious. These small steps can serve as proof of concept, demonstrating the efficacy of a particular policy or approach and building public and political will for further change.

On the other side of complacency sits the frustration that can develop when no tangible progress is made. This is the risk of accelerationism— that is, that the goals are so massive and unlikely, and potentially even legally problematic, that activists achieve absolutely nothing for years and become disaffected for that reason.

DILUTION OF POLICY GOALS

When a group of elected officials or activists initially paints a clear picture of their objective, that objective is clear, due to the recency with which it was developed. One could criticize incrementalism with the argument that when it takes longer to achieve that objective, or when the objective is divided into many small steps to be undertaken one at a time over a longer period, the core objectives of a transformative agenda might get diluted. This could be as a result of people moving in and out of the effort, from changes to the status quo within which the activism is taking place, or simply because of people forgetting what their original goals were as time passes.

However, dilution is not a necessary outcome of incrementalism. With a clear long-term vision and strategic planning, incremental steps can be components of a comprehensive and ambitious road map. The small successes can be opportunities to confirm and reconfirm that the movement is still on the right path, and to adjust as necessary, potentially even making the ultimate goal more precise and beneficial.

REVERSIBILITY OF ACCOMPLISHMENTS

The reversibility objection to incrementalism argues that minor changes can be more easily reversed, especially if they lack widespread support or are seen as experimental. In fact, this concern has already been addressed earlier.

While small changes can theoretically be reversed, so can large changes. Small changes can also be foundational and set precedents for future policy. Moreover, sweeping reforms can be just as vulnerable to rollback, especially if they are polarizing or lack broad consensus. In some sense, it is the larger and more audacious changes that are more likely to end up completely reversed on legal appeal.

PUBLIC PERCEPTION

If we're honest with ourselves, incrementalism also suffers from a deficit when it comes to public perception. A party or politician focusing on incremental changes can be seen as lacking ambition, potentially damaging their reputation or electoral prospects. An activist movement focusing on incrementalism can be seen as boring, or not ambitious enough, and have trouble raising money or generating interest.

This is, in truth, the strongest argument against incrementalism, and it is an argument merely about perception. Public perception is indeed crucial, but effectiveness and long-term impact should be the primary goals. By communicating the broader vision behind incremental steps and demonstrating tangible benefits to constituents, public support can be nurtured and maintained.

While the criticisms of incrementalism have their merit, a nuanced perspective reveals that this approach, when executed with vision and strategy, can yield lasting and meaningful change and is the best approach, as demonstrated by historical achievements and by an analysis of the arguments for or against.

The allure of accelerationism is understandably tempting thanks to its promise of rapid transformation, but history has shown that its outcomes can be unpredictable and destabilizing. The methodical and sustainable path of incrementalism, when embraced, can ensure that reforms are deeply rooted and broadly supported, and importantly, foster an environment where progress builds on itself, ideally securing a foundation for enduring advancement for societies as wholes.

ACKNOWLEDGMENTS

Writing this first book has been quite the journey, and I couldn't have completed it without the support, encouragement, and assistance of many people.

First and foremost, thanks to my family, whose unwavering support and belief in the project has kept the book moving forward even on days where the direction became less clear or a roadblock was reached.

Thanks to my literary agent, Rob Kirkpatrick, for his belief in me and this project, and his help guiding it from a mere passing thought to an idea, a proposal, and eventually to Beacon Press.

Thanks to Joanna Green, my editor, and the entire team at Beacon Press.

I am deeply grateful to my team at *The David Pakman Show*, including John, Pat, and Noah, for suggestions about the concept of this book, research assistance, and endless invaluable ideas.

I also want to acknowledge my entire podcast and video audience over the years for creating the universe of online, independent media, which created the environment that led to thinking about writing a book in the first place.

Lastly, I want to express my gratitude to my readers. Your interest and engagement have made this journey worthwhile. I hope the book provides you with insights and inspiration for your own future political activism.

NOTES

CHAPTER 1: HOW THE UNITED STATES BROKE

1. Juliana Menasce Horowitz et al., "Trends in Income and Wealth Inequality," Social and Demographic Trends Project, Pew Research Center, January 9, 2020, www.pewresearch.org/social-trends/2020/01/09/trends-in-income-and-wealth -inequality.

2. Drew DeSilver, "10 Facts about American Workers," Pew Research Center, August 29, 2019, https://www.pewresearch.org/short-reads/2019/08/29/facts-about -american-workers; Tom McCarthy, "Donald Trump and the Erosion of Democratic Norms in America," *Guardian*, June 2, 2018, www.theguardian.com/us-news /2018/jun/02/trump-department-of-justice-robert-mueller-crisis.

3. "Citizens United v. FEC," FEC.gov, https://www.fec.gov/legal-resources /court-cases/citizens-united-v-fec, accessed April 5, 2024.

4. "White Citizens' Councils (WCC)," Martin Luther King, Jr. Research & Education Institute, Stanford University, https://kinginstitute.stanford.edu/white -citizens-councils-wcc, accessed April 5, 2024.

5. "Competing Visions of America: An Evolving Identity or a Culture Under Attack? Findings from the 2021 American Values Survey," PRRI, November 3, 2021, https://www.prri.org/research/competing-visions-of-america-an-evolving -identity-or-a-culture-under-attack.

6. Gavin Wright, "The Regional Economic Impact of the Civil Rights Act of 1964," *Boston University Law Review* 95 (2015), https://www.bu.edu/bulawreview /files/2015/05/WRIGHT.pdf.

7. Michael D. Dodd et al., "The Political Left Rolls with the Good and the Political Right Confronts the Bad: Connecting Physiology and Cognition to Preferences," *Philosophical Transactions of the Royal Society of London, Series B, Biological Sciences*, US National Library of Medicine, March 5, 2012, www.ncbi.nlm.nih.gov /pmc/articles/PMC3260844.

8. Virgie Hoban, "'Discredit, Disrupt, and Destroy': FBI Records Acquired by the Library Reveal Violent Surveillance of Black Leaders, Civil Rights Organizations," UC Berkeley Library, University of California, Berkeley, January 18, 2021, www.lib.berkeley.edu/about/news/fbi.

9. "'Welfare Queen' Becomes Issue in Reagan Campaign," *New York Times*, February 15, 1976, www.nytimes.com/1976/02/15/archives/welfare-queen
-becomes-issue-in-reagan-campaign-hitting-a-nerve-now.html.

10. Ronald Reagan, "Inaugural Address," Ronald Reagan Presidential Foundation & Institute, January 20, 1981, www.reaganfoundation.org/media/128614
/inaguration.pdf.

11. Richard G. Frank and Sherry A. Glied, "Keep Obamacare to Keep Progress on Treating Opioid Disorders and Mental Illnesses," *The Hill*, September 19, 2017, thehill.com/blogs/pundits-blog/healthcare/313672-keep-obamacare-to-keep
-progress-on-treating-opioid-disorders; Sharon Zhang, "205 Republicans Vote Against Bill to Expand School Mental Health Services," *Truthout*, January 24, 2023, truthout.org/articles/205-republicans-vote-against-bill-to-expand-school-mental
-health-services.

12. "Contract with America," *Encyclopedia Britannica*, September 20, 2023, https://www.britannica.com/event/Contract-with-America.

13. Susan Finley, "Interrupting History: Anti-Intellectualism in the George W. Bush Administration," *Cultural Studies ↔ Critical Methodologies* 9, no. 1 (February 1, 2009): 23–30, https://doi.org/10.1177/1532708608321398.

14. Anthony H. Cordesman, "Intelligence Failures in the Iraq War," Center for Strategic and International Studies, July 16, 2003, www.csis.org/analysis
/intelligence-failures-iraq-war.

15. Matthew Rozsa, "Climate Change Denial Hit Its Stride in the Bush-Cheney Era, Precipitating Today's Climate Disaster," *Salon*, June 19, 2023, www.salon.com/2023/06/19/climate-change-denial-hit-its-stride-in-the-bush
-cheney-era-precipitating-todays-climate-disaster; Jeanne Lenzer, "Bush Says He Will Veto Stem Cell Funding, Despite Vote in Favour in Congress," *British Medical Journal* 334, no. 7606 (June 16, 2007): 1243, doi: 10.1136/bmj.39245.359306.DB.

16. Ewen MacAskill, "George Bush: 'God Told Me to End the Tyranny in Iraq,'" *Guardian*, October 7, 2005, www.theguardian.com/world/2005/oct/07/iraq
.usa.

17. Gregory Krieg, "14 of Trump's Most Outrageous 'Birther' Claims—Half from After 2011," CNN Politics, September 16, 2016, www.cnn.com/2016/09/09
/politics/donald-trump-birther/index.html.

18. Anti-Defamation League, *White Supremacist Propaganda Soars to All-Time High in 2022*, March 8, 2023, www.adl.org/resources/report/white-supremacist
-propaganda-soars-all-time-high-2022.

19. Jennifer Epstein, "Obama Scoffs at People Who Call Him a 'Socialist': 'You Gotta Meet Real Socialists,'" *Politico*, November 19, 2013, www.politico.com/blogs
/politico44/2013/11/obama-scoffs-at-people-who-call-him-a-socialist-you-gotta
-meet-real-socialists-177886.

20. Mark Brewer, "Trump Knows Best: Donald Trump's Rejection of Expertise and the 2020 Presidential Election," *Society*, 2020, https://www.ncbi.nlm.nih.gov
/pmc/articles/PMC7786860.

21. Daniella Silva, "Betsy DeVos to Overhaul Obama-Era Title IX Guidance on Campus Sex Assault," NBC News, September 7, 2017, www.nbcnews.com/news
/us-news/betsy-devos-overhaul-obama-era-guidance-campus-sex-assault-n799471.

22. Juana Summers, "Timeline: How Trump Has Downplayed the Corona-virus Pandemic," NPR, October 2, 2020, www.npr.org/sections/latest-updates -trump-covid-19-results/2020/10/02/919432383/how-trump-has-downplayed-the -coronavirus-pandemic.

23. Julie Hirschfeld Davis, "Rumblings of a 'Deep State' Undermining Trump? It Was Once a Foreign Concept," *New York Times*, March 7, 2017, www.nytimes .com/2017/03/06/us/politics/deep-state-trump.html; David Klepper and Ali Swen-son, "Trump Openly Embraces, Amplifies QAnon Conspiracy Theories," AP News, September 16, 2022, apnews.com/article/technology-donald-trump-conspiracy -theories-government-and-politics-db50c6f709b1706886a876ae6ac298e2.

24. Cayli Baker, "The Trump Administration's Major Environmental Deregula-tions," Brookings Institution, December 15, 2020, www.brookings.edu/articles/the -trump-administrations-major-environmental-deregulations.

25. Megan A. Brown et al., "Echo Chambers, Rabbit Holes, and Ideological Bias: How YouTube Recommends Content to Real Users," Brookings Institution, October 13, 2022, www.brookings.edu/articles/echo-chambers-rabbit-holes-and -ideological-bias-how-youtube-recommends-content-to-real-users.

26. "Fact Sheet: House Republican Proposals Hurt Children, Students, and Borrowers, and Undermine Education," press release, US Department of Educa-tion, April 25, 2023, www.ed.gov/news/press-releases/fact-sheet-house-republican -proposals-hurt-children-students-and-borrowers-and-undermine-education.

27. Gregor Aisch, Jon Huang, and Cecilia Kang, "Dissecting the #PizzaGate Conspiracy Theories," *New York Times*, December 10, 2016, https://www.nytimes .com/interactive/2016/12/10/business/media/pizzagate.html.

28. Brett Barrouquere, "El Paso Shooting Suspect May Have Authored Manifesto Containing White Nationalist Talking Points," Southern Poverty Law Center, August 3, 2019, www.splcenter.org/hatewatch/2019/08/03/el-paso-shooting -suspect-may-have-authored-manifesto-containing-white-nationalist-talking.

29. Jordan M. Foley and Michael W. Wagner, "How Media Consumption Pat-terns Fuel Conspiratorial Thinking," Brookings Institution, May 26, 2020, https:// www.brookings.edu/articles/how-media-consumption-patterns-fuel-conspiratorial -thinking.

CHAPTER 2: WHAT HAPPENED TO CRITICAL THINKING?

1. Jon Henley, "How Finland Starts Its Fight Against Fake News in Primary Schools," *Guardian*, January 29, 2020, https://www.theguardian.com/world/2020 /jan/28/fact-from-fiction-finlands-new-lessons-in-combating-fake-news.

2. Tee Zhuo, "Parliament: Critical Thinking Not Just in Liberal Education, but All Schools Here, Says Faishal," *Straits Times*, October 7, 2019, https://www .straitstimes.com/politics/parliament-critical-thinking-not-just-in-liberal-education -but-all-schools-here-says.

3. Gregor Aisch, Jon Huang, and Cecilia Kang, "Dissecting the #PizzaGate Conspiracy Theories," *New York Times*, December 10, 2016, https://www.nytimes .com/interactive/2016/12/10/business/media/pizzagate.html.

4. Rebecca Hersher, "U.S. Officially Leaving Paris Climate Agreement," NPR, November 3, 2020, https://www.npr.org/2020/11/03/930312701/u-s-officially -leaving-paris-climate-agreement.

5. Antony Blinken, "The United States Officially Rejoins the Paris Agreement," US Department of State, February 19, 2021, https://www.state.gov/the-united -states-officially-rejoins-the-paris-agreement.

6. Glenn Kessler, "A Look at Trump's 'Birther' Statements," *Washington Post*, April 28, 2011, https://www.washingtonpost.com/blogs/fact-checker/post/a-look-at -trumps-birther-statements/2011/04/27/AFeOYb1E_blog.html.

7. Dmitry Erokhin et al., "COVID-19 Conspiracy Theories Discussion on Twitter," *Social Media + Society* 8, no. 4 (October 2022), https://doi.org/10.1177 /20563051221126051.

8. Jemima McEvoy, "3 in 10 Republicans Believe Wacky Conspiracy Theory Trump Will Be 'Reinstated' as President This Year, Poll Shows," *Forbes*, June 9, 2021, https://www.forbes.com/sites/jemimamcevoy/2021/06/09/3-in -10-republicans-believe-wacky-conspiracy-theory-trump-will-be-reinstated-as -president-this-year-poll-shows/?sh=43bod9af3aeb.

9. Alan Rappeport, "Philosophers (and Welders) React to Marco Rubio's Debate Comments," *New York Times*, November 11, 2015, https://archive.nytimes.com /www.nytimes.com/politics/first-draft/2015/11/11/philosophers-and-welders-react -to-marco-rubios-debate-comments.

10. "Here's How the Deficit Performed Under Republican and Democratic Presidents, from Reagan to Trump," PolitiFact, July 23, 2019, https://www .politifact.com/factchecks/2019/jul/29/tweets/republican-presidents-democrats -contribute-deficit.

11. "Here's How the Deficit Performed."

12. Chuck Jones, "Trump's Deficits Are Racing Past Obama's," *Forbes*, February 1, 2020, https://www.forbes.com/sites/chuckjones/2020/02/01/trumps-deficits-are -racing-past-obamas/?sh=71db30164819.

13. Federal Reserve Bank of St. Louis, "Federal Surplus or Deficit [-] as Percent of Gross Domestic Product," https://fred.stlouisfed.org/series /FYFSGDA188S.

14. "How the 1968 Riots Made Agnew's Career," *Baltimore Sun*, April 5, 1998, https://www.baltimoresun.com/1998/04/05/how-the-1968-riots-made-agnews -career.

15. Livia Gershon, "Ronald Reagan v. UC Berkeley," *JSTOR Daily*, April 29, 2023, https://daily.jstor.org/ronald-reagan-v-uc-berkeley.

16. Jared Sharpe, "Republicans Blame Democrats, Antifa and U.S. Capitol Police for Jan. 6 Mayhem, According to New UMass Amherst/WCVB Poll," University of Massachusetts Amherst, April 27, 2021, https://www.umass.edu/news /article/republicans-blame-democrats-antifa-and-us.

17. Daniel Villarreal, "Marjorie Taylor Greene Says Prisons 'Torturing' January 6 Rioters," *Newsweek*, November 5, 2021, https://www.newsweek.com/politics-evil -marjorie-taylor-greene-says-prisons-torturing-january-6-rioters-1646638.

18. Donald Trump, "Mark Milley, who led perhaps the most embarrassing moment . . ." Truth Social, September 22, 2023, https://truthsocial.com/@ realDonaldTrump/posts/111111513207332826.

19. Annie Karni, "Republican Leaders Stand Behind Santos After His Indictment," *New York Times*, May 10, 2023, https://www.nytimes.com/2023/05/10/us /politics/mccarthy-george-santos-congress.html.

20. Martin Pengelly, "Donald Trump Vows to Lock Up Political Enemies If He Returns to White House," *Guardian*, August 30, 2023, https://www.theguardian.com/us-news/2023/aug/30/trump-interview-jail-political-opponents-glenn-beck.

21. Amanda Macias, "Trump and GOP Rep. Gosar Suggest Joint Chiefs Boss Mark Milley Deserves Death," CNBC, September 25, 2023, https://www.cnbc.com/2023/09/25/trump-paul-gosar-suggest-gen-mark-milley-deserves-death.html.

22. "Bush: 'You Are Either with Us, or with the Terrorists,'" *Voice of America*, October 27, 2009, https://www.voanews.com/a/a-13-a-2001-09-21-14-bush-66411197/549664.html.

23. "Dems, GOP Turn Up Heat on Obama over Drones," CBS News, May 8, 2013, https://www.cbsnews.com/news/dems-gop-turn-up-heat-on-obama-over-drones.

24. Jeremy Diamond, "Trump Warns of World War III If Clinton Is Elected," CNN Politics, October 25, 2016, https://www.cnn.com/2016/10/25/politics/donald-trump-hillary-clinton-world-war-iii-syria/index.html.

CHAPTER 3: WHAT ARE FACTS?

1. David W. Angel, "The Four Types of Conversations: Debate, Dialogue, Discourse, and Diatribe," *The Opportune Conflict* (blog), December 28, 2016, https://davidwangel.com/the-opportune-conflict/2016/12/28/the-four-types-of-conversations-debate-dialogue-discourse-and-diatribe.

2. David W. Angel, "When Arguing over Value Issues, Sometimes Facts and Truth Don't Matter," *The Opportune Conflict* (blog), September 23, 2016, https://davidwangel.com/the-opportune-conflict/2016/9/23/when-arguing-over-value-issues-sometimes-facts-and-truth-dont-matter.

3. Amy Mitchell, Jeffrey Gottfried, Michael Barthel, and Nami Sumida, *Distinguishing Between Factual and Opinion Statements in the News*, Pew Research Center, June 18, 2018, https://www.pewresearch.org/journalism/wp-content/uploads/sites/8/2018/06/PJ_2018.06.18_fact-opinion_FINAL.pdf.

4. Ryan Zamarripa, "5 Ways the Trump Administration's Policy Failures Compounded the Coronavirus-Induced Economic Crisis," Center for American Progress, June 3, 2020, https://www.americanprogress.org/article/5-ways-trump-administrations-policy-failures-compounded-coronavirus-induced-economic-crisis.

5. Elliott D. Cohen, "Plato's Prognosis of 'Alternative Fact,'" *Psychology Today*, February 12, 2017, https://www.psychologytoday.com/us/blog/what-would-aristotle-do/201702/plato-s-prognosis-alternative-facts.

6. Amy Lerman and Daniel Acland, "United in States of Dissatisfaction: Confirmation Bias Across the Partisan Divide," *American Politics Research* 48, no. 2 (September 19, 2018): 227–37, https://doi.org/10.1177/1532673x18799274.

7. Story Pennock, "Echo Chambers: How They're Created and How to Avoid Them," Poynter, May 5, 2023, https://www.poynter.org/tfcn/2023/echo-chambers-how-theyre-created-and-how-to-avoid-them.

8. Tovia Smith, "'Dude, I'm Done': When Politics Tears Families and Friendships Apart," NPR, October 27, 2020, https://www.npr.org/2020/10/27/928209548/dude-i-m-done-when-politics-tears-families-and-friendships-apart.

9. Jeff Turrentine, "Climate Misinformation on Social Media Is Undermining Climate Action," Natural Resources Defense Council, April 19, 2022, https://www.nrdc.org/stories/climate-misinformation-social-media-undermining-climate-action.

10. Marilyn A. Brown and Majid Ahmadi, "Would a Green New Deal Add or Kill Jobs?," *Scientific American*, December 17, 2019, https://www.scientificamerican.com/article/would-a-green-new-deal-add-or-kill-jobs1.

11. Pien Huang, "How Ivermectin Became the New Focus of the Anti-Vaccine Movement," NPR, September 19, 2021, https://www.npr.org/sections/health-shots/2021/09/19/1038369557/ivermectin-anti-vaccine-movement-culture-wars.

12. Ingjerd Skafle, Anders Nordahl-Hansen, Daniel S. Quintana, Rolf Wynn, and Elia Gabarron, "Misinformation About COVID-19 Vaccines on Social Media: Rapid Review," *Journal of Medical Internet Research* 24, no. 8 (August 4, 2022), https://doi.org/10.2196/37367.

13. "The Persistence of QAnon in the Post-Trump Era: An Analysis of Who Believes the Conspiracies," PRRI, February 24, 2022, https://www.prri.org/research/the-persistence-of-qanon-in-the-post-trump-era-an-analysis-of-who-believes-the-conspiracies.

14. Neil Postman, *Technopoly: The Surrender of Culture to Technology* (New York: Knopf, 1992).

15. Eric Plutzer, Glenn Branch, and Ann Reid, "Teaching Evolution in U.S. Public Schools: A Continuing Challenge," *Evolution: Education and Outreach* 13, no. 1 (June 9, 2020), https://doi.org/10.1186/s12052-020-00126-8.

16. Kimberlé Crenshaw, "Demarginalizing the Intersection of Race and Sex: A Black Feminist Critique of Antidiscrimination Doctrine, Feminist Theory and Antiracist Politics," *University of Chicago Legal Forum* no. 1, article 8 (1989), http://chicagounbound.uchicago.edu/uclf/vol1989/iss1/8.

17. N'dea Yancey-Bragg, "Nearly 100 Confederate Statues Were Removed in 2020, but Hundreds Remain, New SPLC Data Shows," *USA Today*, February 23, 2021, https://www.usatoday.com/story/news/nation/2021/02/23/historic-number-confederate-statues-were-removed-2020-splc/4556708001.

CHAPTER 4: THE COST OF PRINCIPLES OVER PROBLEMS
1. US Congress, "Southern Manifesto," Congressional Record, 84th Congress, Second Session, vol. 102, part 4 (Washington, DC: Governmental Printing Office, 1956), 4459–60.

2. Barry M. Goldwater, *The Conscience of a Conservative* (New York: Shepherd Books, 1960).

3. Jon Entine, "Climate Change Contrarian: How Green Hysteria Will Hit the US," Pacific Research Institute, May 16, 2008, https://www.pacificresearch.org/climate-change-contrarian-how-green-hysteria-will-hit-the-us.

4. NASA, "Scientific Consensus: Earth's Climate Is Warming," NASA, https://science.nasa.gov/climate-change/scientific-consensus, accessed April 29, 2024.

5. Peter Overby, "NRA: 'Only Thing That Stops a Bad Guy with a Gun Is a Good Guy with a Gun,'" NPR, https://www.npr.org/2012/12/21/167824766/nra-only-thing-that-stops-a-bad-guy-with-a-gun-is-a-good-guy-with-a-gun.

6. Max Fisher, "After Mass Gun Killings, Other Nations Changed Course—to Notable Effect," *New York Times*, May 25, 2022, https://www.nytimes.com/2022/05 /25/world/europe/gun-laws-australia-britain.html.

7. "Guns and Violence Against Women: America's Uniquely Lethal Intimate Partner Violence Problem," Everytown Research and Policy, October 17, 2019, https://everytownresearch.org/report/guns-and-violence-against-women-americas -uniquely-lethal-intimate-partner-violence-problem.

8. National Federation of Independent Business v. Sebelius, 567 U.S. 519 (2012).

9. "McConnell: Healthcare Bill a 'Job Killer,'" UPI, November 22, 2009, https://www.upi.com/Top_News/US/2009/11/22/McConnell-Healthcare-bill -a-job-killer/10751258921249.

10. World Health Organization, "Universal Health Coverage (UHC)," October 5, 2023, https://www.who.int/news-room/fact-sheets/detail/universal-health -coverage-(uhc).

11. Ted Cruz, "Transcript of Sen. Ted Cruz's Filibuster Against Obamacare," *Washington Post*, September 25, 2013, https://www.washingtonpost.com/sf/national /2013/09/25/transcript-sen-ted-cruzs-filibuster-against-obamacare.

12. Louis Jacobson, "Sarah Silverman stated on May 22, 2015 in a social media post: Says Sen. Rand Paul, R-Ky., has stated that supporting the 'Right to health care . . . means you believe in slavery,'" PolitiFact, May 27, 2015, https://www .politifact.com/factchecks/2015/may/27/sarah-silverman/did-rand-paul-equate -right-health-care-slavery.

13. Nancy Marshall, "Podcasting Is Growing for a Reason—Don't Miss Out on That Growth," *Forbes*, January 18, 2023, https://www.forbes.com/sites /forbesagencycouncil/2023/01/17/podcasting-is-growing-for-a-reason-dont-miss -out-on-that-growth/?sh=7dd3759b42a7.

14. Emma Grey Ellis, "Welcome to the Age of the Hour-Long YouTube Video," *Wired*, November 12, 2018, https://www.wired.com/story/youtube-video -extra-long.

CHAPTER 5: WHY CHOOSE LEFTISM?

1. F. Martela, B. Greve, B. Rothstein, and J. Saari, *The Nordic Exceptionalism: What Explains Why the Nordic Countries Are Constantly Among the Happiest in the World*, World Happiness Report, March 20, 2020, https://worldhappiness.report /ed/2020/the-nordic-exceptionalism-what-explains-why-the-nordic-countries-are -constantly-among-the-happiest-in-the-world.

2. "Corruption Perceptions Index 2023," Transparency International, 2023, https://www.transparency.org/en/cpi/2023.

3. David Nikel, "Nordic Countries Are the World's Safest, New Report Reveals," *Forbes*, November 18, 2019, https://www.forbes.com/sites/davidnikel /2019/11/18/nordic-countries-are-the-worlds-safest-new-report-reveals/?sh= 36720a88ffd7.

4. "What We Can Learn From Norway's Prison System: Rehabilitation and Recidivism," First Step Alliance, November 26, 2023, https://www.firststepalliance .org/post/norway-prison-system-lessons.

5. "Ease of Doing Business Rankings," World Bank, https://archive.doingbusiness.org/en/rankings, accessed April 29, 2024.

6. Klaus Schwab and Saadia Zahidi, *The Global Competitiveness Report Special Edition 2020*, World Economic Forum, 2020, https://www3.weforum.org/docs/WEF_TheGlobalCompetitivenessReport2020.pdf.

7. Colm Fulton and Supantha Mukherjee, "Focus: How Sweden Became the Silicon Valley of Europe," Reuters, August 11, 2021, https://www.reuters.com/business/finance/how-sweden-became-silicon-valley-europe-2021-08-11.

8. "Happy Workers Are 13% More Productive," University of Oxford, October 24, 2019, https://www.ox.ac.uk/news/2019-10-24-happy-workers-are-13-more-productive.

9. Noah Berger and Peter Fisher, "A Well-Educated Workforce Is Key to State Prosperity," Economic Policy Institute, August 22, 2013, https://www.epi.org/publication/states-education-productivity-growth-foundations.

10. Louise Lee, "The Case for a Danish-Style Safety Net," Stanford Graduate School of Business, March 28, 2018, https://www.gsb.stanford.edu/insights/case-danish-style-safety-net.

11. OECD, "Sweden," https://www.oecd.org/migration/integration-indicators-2012/keyindicatorsbycountry/name,218347,en.htm, accessed April 29, 2024; "Immigrants and Norwegian-Born to Immigrant Parents, 1 January 2016," Statistics Norway, archived September 18, 2019, at the Wayback Machine, accessed April 29, 2024.

12. "Uruguay's Record-Setting Economic Growth Streak," *Economist*, March 28, 2018, https://www.economist.com/the-americas/2018/03/28/uruguays-record-setting-economic-growth-streak.

13. Brian Winter, "What Uruguay Can Teach Us," *Americas Quarterly*, January 13, 2023, https://www.americasquarterly.org/article/what-uruguay-can-teach-us.

14. Brian Fowler and Emiliana Vegas, "How Uruguay Implemented Its Computer Science Education Program," Brookings Institution, March 12, 2021, https://www.brookings.edu/articles/how-uruguay-implemented-its-computer-science-education-program.

15. Kay Bond, ed., *Building Up the National Integrated Health System*, World Health Organization, October 7, 2015, https://www.who.int/publications/i/item/WHO-HIS-HGF-CaseStudy-15.10.

16. Soledad Quartucci, "Uruguay's Road to Development," Latina Republic, May 15, 2023, https://latinarepublic.com/2023/05/15/uruguays-road-to-development.

17. World Bank, "Poverty and Equity Brief: Latin America and the Caribbean, Uruguay," April 2023, https://databankfiles.worldbank.org/public/ddpext_download/poverty/987B9C90-CB9F-4D93-AE8C-750588BF00QA/current/Global_POVEQ_URY.pdf.

18. "GDP Growth (Annual %)—Portugal," Open Data, World Bank, https://data.worldbank.org/indicator/NY.GDP.MKTP.KD.ZG?end=2019&locations=PT&start=2016, accessed April 29, 2024.

19. "Portugal Public Debt," FocusEconomics, 2022, https://www.focus-economics.com/country-indicator/portugal/public-debt.

20. "Government Approves Greatest Rise Ever of the Minimum Wage," news release, Government of Portugal, November 9, 2023, https://www.portugal.gov.pt /en/gc23/communication/news-item?i=government-approves-greatest-rise-ever-of -the-minimum-wage.

21. Vincent Bevins, "Where Progressives Are Winning," *Atlantic*, October 7, 2019, https://www.theatlantic.com/international/archive/2019/10/portugal -election-progressives-left-winning/599518.

22. Arthur Neslen, "Portugal Runs for Four Days Straight on Renewable Energy Alone," *Guardian*, May 18, 2016, https://www.theguardian.com/environment /2016/may/18/portugal-runs-for-four-days-straight-on-renewable-energy-alone.

23. Paul Luckman, "54% of Portugal's Electricity Is Now Generated by Renewable Energy," *Portugal News*, September 30, 2023, https://www.theportugalnews .com/news/2023-09-30/54-of-portugals-electricity-is-now-generated-by-renewable -energy/81840.

24. "Increase in Passengers Using Public Transport," *Portugal News*, November 12, 2023, https://www.theportugalnews.com/news/2023-11-12/increase-in -passengers-using-public-transport/83175.

25. Anna Jaquiery, "New Zealand: Changing the Conversation on Well-Being," International Monetary Fund, January 26, 2022, https://www.imf.org/en/News /Articles/2022/01/26/cf-new-zealand-changing-the-conversation-on-well-being.

26. "Climate Change Response (Zero Carbon) Amendment Act 2019," Ministry for the Environment, April 5, 2021, https://environment.govt.nz/acts-and -regulations/acts/climate-change-response-amendment-act-2019.

27. Praveen Menon, "New Zealand's PM Ardern Acts to Tighten Gun Laws Further, Six Months After Attack," Reuters, September 12, 2019, https://www.reu ters.com/article/idUSKCN1VY08S.

28. "How Jacinda Ardern Tackled Public Health Crises in New Zealand," Harvard T. H. Chan School of Public Health, November 21, 2023, https://www .hsph.harvard.edu/news/features/how-jacinda-ardern-tackled-public-health-crises -in-new-zealand.

29. Lothar Funk, "Chancellor Proposes Agenda 2010 to Revive Economy," Eurofound, March 30, 2003, https://www.eurofound.europa.eu/en/resources/article /2003/chancellor-proposes-agenda-2010-revive-economy.

30. "GDP—Germany," Open Data, World Bank, https://data.worldbank.org /indicator/NY.GDP.MKTP.CD?end=2007&locations=DE&start=2003, accessed April 29, 2024.

31. "Unemployment—Germany," Open Data, World Bank, https://data.world-bank.org/indicator/SL.UEM.TOTL.ZS?locations=DE, accessed April 29, 2024.

32. "Trade Summary for Germany 2003," World Integrated Trade Solution, https://wits.worldbank.org/CountryProfile/en/Country/DEU/Year/2003/Summary text, accessed April 29, 2024.

33. "Renewable Energy Sources Act (Erneuerbare-Energien-Gesetz EEG)," IEA, October 8, 2014, https://www.iea.org/policies/3858-renewable-energy -sources-act-erneuerbare-energien-gesetz-eeg.

34. "Schroeder: Germany Needs Immigrants," CNN, December 23, 2000, https://www.cnn.com/2000/WORLD/europe/germany/12/23/schroeder .immigration.

35. "At 96.2%, Kerala Tops Literacy Rate Chart; Andhra Pradesh Worst Performer at 66.4%," *Economic Times*, September 7, 2020, https://economictimes .indiatimes.com/news/politics-and-nation/at-96-2-kerala-tops-literacy-rate-chart -andhra-pradesh-worst-performer-at-66-4/articleshow/77978682.cms.

36. A. Madore et al., "Positive Outlier: Health Outcomes in Kerala, India over Time," Harvard Business Publishing, 2018, https://www.globalhealthdelivery.org /publications/positive-outlier-health-outcomes-kerala-india-over-time.

37. Deepak Johnson, "Land Reforms and Change: Illustrations from Villages in Central Kerala," Foundation for Agrarian Studies, July 26, 2023, https://fas.org.in /land-reforms-villages-central-kerala-namboodiripad.

38. "UP Literacy Rate Poor [*sic*] Than National Average: Report," *Hindustan Times*, September 8, 2020, https://www.hindustantimes.com/education/up-literacy -rate-poor-than-national-average-report/story-04cd30glcG2IchqkB0TLaJ.html; Swagata Yadavar and Shreya Raman, "Here's Why India Has One of the Highest Rates of Infant Mortality in the World," *The Wire*, January 10, 2020, https://thewire .in/health/infant-deaths-india; Saher Ronaq, "Gender Inequality in Rajasthan: Breaking Barriers for Women's Rights," Legal Research and Analysis, April 22, 2023, https://legalresearchandanalysis.com/gender-inequality-in-rajasthan-break/.

39. Wesley Lowery, "91% of the Time the Better-Financed Candidate Wins. Don't Act Surprised," *Washington Post*, April 4, 2014, https://www.washingtonpost .com/news/the-fix/wp/2014/04/04/think-money-doesnt-matter-in-elections-this -chart-says-youre-wrong.

40. "The Impact of Voter Suppression on Communities of Color," fact sheet, Brennan Center for Justice, January 10, 2022, https://www.brennancenter.org/our -work/research-reports/impact-voter-suppression-communities-color.

41. "Georgia Removed Nearly 190K Voters from Rolls, 305K Remain Inactive," FOX 5 Atlanta, September 13, 2023, https://www.fox5atlanta.com/news /georgia-removed-nearly-voters-from-rolls-inactive-status.

42. Nicholas Riccardi, "Here's the Reality Behind Trump's Claims About Mail Voting," AP News, September 30, 2020, https://apnews.com /article/virus-outbreak-joe-biden-election-2020-donald-trump-elections -3e8170c3348ce3719d4bc7182146b582.

CHAPTER 6: HOW TO FIGHT AGAINST A MOVEMENT THAT HAS NO POLICY

1. Gillian Brockell, "She Was Stereotyped as 'the Welfare Queen.' The Truth Was More Disturbing, a New Book Says," *Washington Post*, May 21, 2019, https:// www.washingtonpost.com/history/2019/05/21/she-was-stereotyped-welfare-queen -truth-was-more-disturbing-new-book-says.

2. Sahil Kapur, "Trump Says Obamacare Must Die. Biden Says He'll Make It into 'Bidencare,'" NBC News, October 23, 2020, https://www.nbcnews.com /politics/2020-election/trump-says-obamacare-must-die-biden-says-he-ll-make -n1244454.

3. Darlene Superville, "Trump Paints Apocalyptic Portrait of Life in US Under Biden," AP News, October 29, 2020, https://apnews.com/article/election-2020-joe -biden-donald-trump-police-economy-3082b995c1fd89129671b245797bc902.

4. Ron Filipkowski, "Guy at Trump's speech …," Twitter, September 21, 2023, https://twitter.com/RonFilipkowski/status/1704813604837405026.

5. Elizabeth Landers, "Spicer: Trump's Tweets Are Official Statements," CNN, June 6, 2017, https://www.cnn.com/2017/06/06/politics/trump-tweets-official -statements/index.html.

6. Bradley Jones, "Increasing Share of Americans Favor a Single Government Program to Provide Health Care Coverage," Pew Research Center, September 29, 2020, https://www.pewresearch.org/short-reads/2020/09/29/increasing-share-of -americans-favor-a-single-government-program-to-provide-health-care-coverage.

7. Gaby Galvin, "About 7 in 10 Voters Favor a Public Health Insurance Op- tion," Morning Consult Pro, March 24, 2021.

8. Domenico Montanaro, "Poll: Majority Want to Keep Abortion Legal, but They Also Want Restrictions," NPR, June 7, 2019, https://www.npr.org/2019/06 /07/730183531/poll-majority-want-to-keep-abortion-legal-but-they-also-want -restrictions.

9. Hannah Hartig, "About Six-in-Ten Americans Say Abortion Should Be Legal in All or Most Cases," Pew Research Center, June 13, 2022, https://www .pewresearch.org/short-reads/2022/06/13/about-six-in-ten-americans-say-abortion -should-be-legal-in-all-or-most-cases-2.

10. "U.S. Public Continues to Favor Legal Abortion, Oppose Overturning *Roe v. Wade*," Pew Research Center, August 29, 2019, https://www.pewresearch .org/politics/2019/08/29/u-s-public-continues-to-favor-legal-abortion-oppose -overturning-roe-v-wade.

11. "U.S. Support for Same-Sex Marriage Matches Record High," Gallup, June 1, 2020, https://news.gallup.com/poll/311672/support-sex-marriage-matches -record-high.aspx.

12. "Top Frustrations with Tax System: Sense That Corporations, Wealthy Don't Pay Fair Share," Pew Research Center, April 14, 2017, https://www.pew research.org/politics/2017/04/14/top-frustrations-with-tax-system-sense-that -corporations-wealthy-dont-pay-fair-share.

13. "Poll: Two-Thirds of Voters Say Billionaires Should Pay a Wealth Tax," *The Hill*, February 26, 2020, https://thehill.com/hilltv/what-americas-thinking/484771 -poll-67-of-voters-believe-billionaires-should-pay-wealth-tax.

14. Howard Schneider and Chris Kahn, "Majority of Americans Favor Wealth Tax on Very Rich: Reuters/Ipsos Poll," Reuters, January 10, 2020, https://www .reuters.com/article/idUSKBN1Z9140.

15. Alec Tyson and Brian Kennedy, "Two-Thirds of Americans Think Gov- ernment Should Do More on Climate," Pew Research Center, June 23, 2020, https://www.pewresearch.org/science/2020/06/23/two-thirds-of-americans-think -government-should-do-more-on-climate.

16. Anthony Leiserowitz et al., "Climate Change in the American Mind—Sep- tember 2021," Yale Program on Climate Change Communication, November 18, 2021, https://climatecommunication.yale.edu/publications/climate-change-in-the -american-mind-september-2021.

17. "Nearly 3 out of 4 Support Raising Legal Age to Buy Any Gun, Quinnipiac University National Poll Finds; Support for Assault Weapons Ban Hits a Low," Quinnipiac University, June 8, 2022, https://poll.qu.edu/poll-release?releaseid= 3848; "Guns," Gallup, April 2019, https://news.gallup.com/poll/1645/guns.aspx; "Bipartisan Support for Expanded Background Checks on Gun Sales," US Politics

and Policy, Pew Research Center, August 13, 2015, https://www.pewresearch.org
/politics/2015/08/13/continued-bipartisan-support-for-expanded-background
-checks-on-gun-sales.

18. Chauncey DeVega, "Election Guru Rachel Bitecofer: Democrats Face
'10-Alarm Fire' After Virginia Debacle," *Salon*, November 12, 2021, https://www
.salon.com/2021/11/12/guru-rachel-bitecofer-democrats-face-10-alarm-fire-after
-virginia-debacle.

19. "There's Something Very Wrong with These Trump Supporters," *The
David Pakman Show*, September 21, 2023, YouTube video, 2:14, https://www.you
tube.com/watch?v=ra7npaM9Nyw.

CHAPTER 7: WHY DOES THE RIGHT KEEP WINNING?

1. Frank Newport, "U.S. Public Opinion and the $3.5 Trillion Senate Budget
Plan," Gallup, August 13, 2021, https://news.gallup.com/opinion/polling-matters
/353582/public-opinion-trillion-senate-budget-plan.aspx.

2. "Virginia Gubernatorial Debate," C-SPAN, September 28, 2021, https://
www.c-span.org/video/?c4979586/user-clip-terry-mcauliffe-i-parents-telling
-schools-teach.

3. Josh Hawley, "Supreme Court Nominee Judge Jackson's Soft-on-Crime
Sentences Are Disturbing," Fox News, March 21, 2022, https://www.foxnews
.com/opinion/supreme-court-nominee-judge-jacksons-crime-sentences-sen-josh
-hawley.

4. Michael Li, Yurij Rudensky, and Laura Royden, "Extreme Gerrymandering
and the 2018 Midterm," Brennan Center for Justice, March 23, 2018, https://www
.brennancenter.org/our-work/research-reports/extreme-gerrymandering-2018
-midterm.

5. For some examples refuting right-wing arguments, see, for example, Canadian Centre for Ethics in Sport, "Literature Review Does Not Support Bans on
Transgender Women Athletes," November 3, 2022, https://cces.ca/news/literature
-review-does-not-support-bans-transgender-women-athletes; Shoshana K. Gold-
berg, "Fair Play: The Importance of Sports Participation for Transgender Youth,"
Center for American Progress, February 8, 2021, https://www.americanprogress
.org/article/fair-play/; Amira Hasenbush, Andrew R. Flores, and Jody L. Herman,
"Gender Identity Nondiscrimination Laws in Public Accommodations: A Review
of Evidence Regarding Safety and Privacy in Public Restrooms, Locker Rooms, and
Changing Rooms," *Sexuality Research and Social Policy* 16 (2019), 70–83, https://link
.springer.com/article/10.1007/s13178-018-0335-z.

6. Claire Carlson, "Does Rural America Have Outsized Influence on the
Electoral College?," Daily Yonder, January 17, 2024, https://dailyyonder.com/rural
-america-influence-on-electoral-college/2024/01/17/.

7. "Agreement Among the States to Elect the President by National Popular
Vote," National Popular Vote!, https://www.nationalpopularvote.com/written
-explanation, accessed April 29, 2024.

8. Tom Norton, "Fact Check: Were Only Trump Supporters Arrested for 2020
Election Fraud?" *Newsweek*, August 4, 2022, https://www.newsweek.com/fact-check
-were-only-trump-supporters-arrested-2020-election-fraud-1730592.

CHAPTER 8: HOW TO (RESPONSIBLY) CONSUME MEDIA

1. Shanto Iyengar and Kyu S. Hahn, "Red Media, Blue Media: Evidence of Ideological Selectivity in Media Use," *Journal of Communication* 59, no. 1 (2009): 19–39, https://psycnet.apa.org/record/2009-04494-002.

2. Rachel Bitecofer, *The Unprecedented 2016 Presidential Election* (Cham, Switzerland: Palgrave, 2018), 36–38, 48.

3. John Hermann, "Who's Responsible When Extremists Get a Platform?" *New York Times Magazine*, December 13, 2016, https://www.nytimes.com/2016/12/13/magazine/whos-responsible-when-extremists-get-a-platform.html.

4. Joe Stumpe and Monica Davey, "Abortion Doctor Shot to Death in Kansas Church," *New York Times*, May 31, 2009, https://www.nytimes.com/2009/06/01/us/01tiller.html.

5. Campbell Robertson, Christopher Mele, and Sabrina Tavernise, "11 Killed in Synagogue Massacre; Suspect Charged with 29 Counts," *New York Times*, October 27, 2018, https://www.nytimes.com/2018/10/27/us/active-shooter-pittsburgh-synagogue-shooting.html.

6. Joel Achenbach, "A Conspiracy Theory about George Soros and a Migrant Caravan Inspired Horror," *Washington Post*, October 28, 2018, https://www.washingtonpost.com/national/a-conspiracy-theory-about-george-soros-and-a-migrant-caravan-inspired-horror/2018/10/28/52df587e-dae6-11e8-b732-3c72cbf131f2_story.html.

7. "What We Can Learn from Finland," Center for an Informed Public, March 1, 2023, https://www.cip.uw.edu/2023/03/01/finland-media-literacy.

8. "6.8 Media Literacy and Safe Use of New Media," Sweden, YouthWiki, European Commission, November 28, 2023, https://national-policies.eacea.ec.europa.eu/youthwiki/chapters/sweden/68-media-literacy-and-safe-use-of-new-media; "About the Dutch Media Literacy Network," Netwerk Mediawijsheid, https://netwerkmediawijsheid.nl/over-ons/about-dutch-media-literacy-network/, accessed July 6, 2024.

9. Sydney Schaedel, "Did the Pope Endorse Trump?" FactCheck.org, October 24, 2016, https://www.factcheck.org/2016/10/did-the-pope-endorse-trump.

CHAPTER 9: WHAT ELSE CAN WE DO?

1. "Twitter Politics 'Experts' Often Do Nothing for Change," *The David Pakman Show*, March 10, 2020, YouTube, https://www.youtube.com/watch?v=c-aT_KBfht4.

2. "Economic Well-Being of U.S. Households in 2022 Fact Sheet," Federal Reserve, https://www.federalreserve.gov/newsevents/pressreleases/files/other20230522a1.pdf, accessed April 29, 2024.

3. Rosabeth Moss Kanter, "Ted Kennedy's Leadership Lessons," *Harvard Business Review*, August 28, 2009, https://hbr.org/2009/08/ted-kennedys-leadership-lessons.

INDEX

dark money, 90
The David Pakman Show, 1, 104, 135
debate, 46, 54
debt and deficit, 33–35
debt defaults, coordinated, 157–58
deepfakes, 59
"defund the police" movement, 117
democracy, 10
Democratic Party election strategies: difficulties facing "do-nothing" Republicans, 109–10, 113; engaging and educating, 111–12; explaining connection of votes to real-world circumstances, 112; highlighting consequences of inaction, 111; introducing critical thinking and media literacy sooner, 112–13; message discipline and consistency, 110–11; Republican abandonment of policy, 102–5, 109; strengthening public education, 112
Denmark, 4, 75–78
desegregation, 11–12
digital activism, 154–56
direct actions activism, 160–61
discourse, 46
disenfranchisement, 5
diversion and deflection, echo chambers for, 52
doubt, 50

early voting, 126
echo chambers of misinformation: climate change, 51; COVID-19, vaccines, and treatments, 51–52; to divert and deflect attention, 52; and erosion of societal cohesion, 50–51; Internet age and, 144; to legitimize policy decisions, 53; to rally the base, 52–53; rise of, 6; voter eligibility and polls, 95
economic freedom and climate change, 66
economic interventions activism, 159
educational systems: decimation of, 23; failing, 10; Kerala state, India, 87; strengthening public education,

112; as vaccine for misinformation, 59–60
Eisenhower, Dwight D., 168–69
election outcomes, and critical thinking skills, 29
election strategies, Democratic Party. *See* Democratic Party election strategies
Electoral College, 92–93, 121–23
electoral system, 90–96; activism and incremental changes, 169–71; Electoral College, 92–93, 121–23; gerrymandering, 95–96; primaries, 93–94; systems of voting, 91–92; voter suppression, 94–95, 125–27
elites, and anti-intellectualism, 16, 17–18, 19, 20
employment: and health care, 154; and political engagement, 152–54; strategic mass absences from work, 157
End Citizens United, 90
Enlightenment, 48, 55
environmental policy preferences, in US, 108
environmental regulation, 53
extremism, platforming of, 134–36

fact-checking, 145
facts *vs.* opinions: about, 45–50; earlier civilizations and birth of debate, 54; exploiting confusion between, 50–51; in the industrial and modern ages, 55; Middle Ages, religion, and science, 54; in the postmodern era, 56; in Renaissance and Enlightenment, 55. *See also* echo chambers of misinformation
false equivalence, 28
family values, 41–43
fear-mongering, 11–12, 110, 115
Federal Election Campaign Act (FECA) of 1971, 89
filibuster, 123–24
Finland, 26, 75–78, 143
first past the post (FPTP) electoral system, 91, 92

ABOUT THE AUTHOR

David Pakman is a political commentator and media personality, most well-known for *The David Pakman Show*. With years of experience, David has cultivated a substantial following across multiple platforms. His show is recognized for its in-depth coverage of contemporary political issues, blending factual reporting with insightful commentary.

Born in Buenos Aires, Argentina, David moved to the United States in his early childhood. He earned a degree in economics and communication from the University of Massachusetts Amherst, where he began to develop his passion for media and politics. David holds an MBA from Bentley University in Waltham, Massachusetts. David's unique perspective, shaped by his background, allows him to approach political discourse with a nuanced and global view.

In addition to his work on *The David Pakman Show*, David is a frequent guest on national news programs and has contributed to numerous publications. His expertise spans a wide range of topics, from economic policy to technology and media.

When he's not in front of a camera, David is an avid traveler and amateur chef.